An Economist Goes to the Game

AN ECONOMIST GOES TO THE GAME

HOW TO THROW AWAY $580 MILLION AND OTHER SURPRISING INSIGHTS FROM THE ECONOMICS OF SPORTS

◆

PAUL OYER

Yale
UNIVERSITY PRESS

New Haven and London

Published with assistance from the foundation established in memory of
Amasa Stone Mather of the Class of 1907, Yale College.

Yale University Press books may be purchased in quantity for
educational, business, or promotional use. For information, please e-mail
sales.press@yale.edu (U.S. office) or sales@yaleup.co.uk (U.K. office).

Set in Gotham and Adobe Garamond types by
Integrated Publishing Solutions.
Printed in the United States of America.

ISBN 978-0-300-21824-4 (hardcover : alk. paper)
Library of Congress Control Number: 2021949772
A catalogue record for this book is available from the British Library.

This paper meets the requirements of ANSI/NISO Z39.48-1992
(Permanence of Paper).

10 9 8 7 6 5 4 3 2

For my father, Calvin Oyer,
who helped develop my loves of sports and learning

Contents

Prologue

On the evening of June 13, 1997, tens of millions of people around the world were glued to their television sets. Twenty-eight seconds remained on the clock in the sixth game of the NBA Finals between the dynastic Chicago Bulls, who led the series three games to two, and the long-suffering Utah Jazz. The game was tied, and the Bulls were huddling, planning the play they would use to take the lead and the NBA championship. Michael Jordan, the Bulls' star, later recalled: "When Phil [Jackson, coach of the Bulls] drew up the play at the end, everybody in the gym, everybody on TV, knew it was coming to me." Jordan was the best player in the league, maybe the best in NBA history, and he had won game 1 for the Bulls with a last-second shot. According to a teammate, the plan on that play was to "give the ball to Michael and get out of the way."[1] When the game restarted, Jordan had the ball and made a move to the basket as though he were going to take a shot—but, covered by two Utah players, he dished the ball to Steve Kerr instead. Kerr, now famous as the coach of another dynasty (the Golden State Warriors of the 2010s), was then a decent NBA guard best known as an accurate shooter. After taking Jordan's pass, Kerr sank a seventeen-foot jump shot to give the Bulls a lead they would not lose.

The Moroccan-born middle-distance runner Rashid Ramzi became a citizen of Bahrain and subsequently brought athletic glory to that island country's one million people. Shortly after becoming a

1

citizen, Ramzi took the world of track and field by storm with victories in the 800-meter and 1,500-meter runs at the Helsinki world championships in 2005. More important, he brought Bahrain its first Olympic gold medal (in fact, its first Olympic medal of any kind) by winning the 1,500-meter race in Beijing in 2008. But his glory didn't last long. Ramzi had to give back his gold medal after a retest in 2009 of his Olympic blood sample showed he had used EPO-CERA, a banned substance meant to help people with kidney problems but also used by cyclists, sprinters, and other athletes to create extra red blood cells.[2]

A twenty-three-year-old South Korean named Jeongeun Lee6 burst onto the golf scene in June 2019, winning the U.S. Women's Open and a $1 million prize. That's not a typo in her name; she goes by "Lee6" because there are so many Lees in the Korean LPGA that it is difficult to keep track of them all. Lee6's victory marked yet another milestone in Korean domination of women's golf.[3]

These three events may seem like a random collection of sports-page headlines and highlights. No doubt they brought joy and excitement to the Bulls, Ramzi (at least initially), Lee6, and their respective fans. But a common thread runs more subtly through these examples: we can look at all of them through the lens of economics. You could even say each is driven by economics. Economic forces drove the participants' choices and strategies in all three examples. Jordan was an amazing player to watch, but his pass to Kerr showed that Jordan also had a grasp of game theory. Ramzi spent his life becoming an elite athlete but at some point realized he could get to the very top of his sport only if he gave in to the prisoner's dilemma. And Lee6's million-dollar payday was the product of growing up in a country with a high savings rate and limited opportunities for women in the labor market.

ESPN doesn't explain these events as natural outcomes of economics. But having researched and taught economics since before Jeongeun Lee6 was born, I believe that all great athletes (well, most of them anyway) and fans are also sound economists. They have to understand how to make investments, how to choose strategies, and how to resolve trade-offs that separate champions from also-rans.

I could not have been Michael Jordan no matter how hard I tried. But Michael Jordan could not have become the (arguably) greatest player of all time without understanding strategy, which in turn relies on economic principles. He had to know the point at which the costs of driving to the hoop one more time outweighed the benefits. All else being equal, Jordan should have taken every shot; he was the best player on the court. But all else is not equal. In equilibrium, opponents guarded Jordan more closely than they guarded Kerr. If they had known that Jordan would take every shot, all five Jazz players would have swarmed him. To truly maximize his talents, the Bulls had to use them just the right amount. That trade-off between taking the shot himself and passing to Kerr was an economic decision that Jordan, through endless practice, coaching, and game experience, knew how to optimize.

Ramzi also had amazing natural athletic talent, which he developed through exhaustive training. It made him one of the best runners in the world. But it probably wasn't enough; he would not have won a gold medal solely through his talent and effort. He faced strong incentives to use banned substances to give himself the extra boost he needed. Although he ended up being caught and disgraced, he took a rational risk to get a huge economic payoff in both money and fame. And because all his top opponents were also taking banned substances, he had no choice if he wanted to make it to the top.

Lee6 was the product of strong economic forces, as well. She grew up in a country with an intense education system, an emphasis on skill development in childhood, and limited labor-market opportunities for talented women. So she focused her investments on developing golf skills. It was a risky bet, but it paid off.

Economics won't make you a great tennis or soccer player, but it answers some of the questions that sports fans ask every day. Should I encourage my kid to try to get a college athletic scholarship (a real one, that is, not the kind people buy)? Why do major sports figures make so much money? Why do NBA teams give players multiyear contracts that guarantee them millions of dollars per year even if they get injured or stop playing well? Why would a pitcher throw the same pitch twice in a row when mixing up pitches is the key to keeping batters off-balance?

In addition to tackling these questions internal to the game, I also hope to shed light on some aspects of public policy. Why do cities build stadiums with public funds, usually with large cost overruns, when the same cities are unable to provide basic services? Are ticket scalpers good or bad? Why can't you get a ticket to a playoff game at a reasonable price?

Along the way, we'll meet people whose lives are driven by both sports and economics. Bobby Estalella was a marginal catcher who hung on in Major League Baseball with the help of unnatural substances; Amy Stephens was a schoolteacher in suburban Atlanta who built a ticket empire after a random event forced her to change one evening's entertainment plans; Tina Weirather was a downhill skier who hails from the greatest per capita sports country in the world (and also the dominant country in producing false teeth). Each of these three people made choices based on the economic forces they faced—the costs and benefits of the opportunities in front of them. All of them had to adjust their plans when the competitive markets in which they were successful evolved in new and more challenging directions.

Though I hope this book will get readers interested in the academic side of sports economics, that is not my main goal. As an economist who loves to play and watch sports, I have written primarily about the economics in doing those things. This book is for sports fans and players, from casual to professional. I focus much less on owners and the many others who make money from sports—such as broadcasters, agents, and advertisers—except as their decisions affect fans and players.

Sports are meant to be fun and relaxing, mostly. I gather that not everybody feels the same is true of economics. I hope you will begin to see, however, as we visit bleachers, broadcast booths, playing fields, and other arenas, that economics too has its entertaining side. Just as you don't need to spend countless hours in the gym to appreciate Michael Jordan's jump shot (or Steve Kerr's), you don't need to master complex equations to enjoy contemplating the insights that economics can give you.

And, just maybe, you will never watch or play a game the same way again.

1

Should You Help Your Kid Become a Pro Athlete?

The sun is setting on Hoover Park one afternoon in April. Hengehold Truck Rental has taken the field for one final stand in a Palo Alto Little League opening-day game. Masonic Lodge, having fallen behind after making roughly fifteen errors in the fourth inning, comes to bat with one last shot to take back the lead. With runners on first and second, the team's star player strides to the plate.

The tension mounts. No more than two of Hengehold's outfielders are picking their noses. Many of the parents watching from the rickety bleachers have looked up from their phones. The pitcher rears and fires a fastball down the middle . . . and David Oyer (my then-twelve-year-old son) crushes it over the left-field fence for a game-winning home run. He jogs around the bases with his fist in the air as though he's just won the World Series, as any self-respecting Little Leaguer would. His teammates mob him at the plate. Masonic Lodge has won its first game of the year.

That game still stands as a highlight in his short career as a star of youth baseball. Both David, whose athletic glory peaked in that final season of Little League, and I, taking vicarious pride in my children's sporting accomplishments the way all overinvolved fathers do, remember the moment as if it were yesterday. It's a safe bet that for the rest of his life David will also remember his first-ever pitching ap-

SHOULD YOU HELP YOUR KID BECOME A PRO ATHLETE?

pearance, when as a nine-year-old he struck out a kid who would eventually become a Stanford varsity pitcher and pro prospect. It's equally likely that I will never forget my only career home run, in the final year of my lengthy stint on the Park ShopRite squad in the Nutley, New Jersey, Little League.

David (now a lawyer) and I are not alone in reliving these moments. Youth sports are a cherished memory for more people than might care to admit it. One reason that is the case, of course, is that sports are fun, and rational humans are utility maximizing—they choose to do the things that bring them the most happiness. Playing sports when one is young, just like going to a movie or an amusement park, increases many people's utility. People "consume" sports participation because they enjoy it.

But there is a second consideration here: youth sports can help develop skills like coordination, teamwork, and decision-making. Think of an eight-year-old point guard who has to learn to dribble, direct an offense, and choose which of her teammates to pass to on every possession—as well as learn that even if she thinks she's the team's best player, if she shoots the ball every time down the floor, her team won't win. Playing basketball might make her smarter, more physically adept, and more sociable—all valuable skills that should contribute to her success and happiness in the future. Parents who consider these factors when they sign their children up for teams see organized sports as an "investment." So youth sports are two kinds of goods in one: a consumption good, like a can of soda or a magazine, and an investment good, like a share of stock or a college education.

How Should Your Kids Spend Their Childhoods?

People often think economics is the study of money, but it's not. It is the study of *scarce resources*. Just as societies have to figure out how best to use scarce resources like water, meat, and clean air, so people have to decide how to spend their limited time, money, and energy. When we wonder how much time kids should devote to sports, we are confronting an economics problem.

Youth is one of the most valuable resources you will ever possess. To use it efficiently, you need to prepare for the rest of your life while having enough fun to avoid looking back with regret. Failure to strike the right balance in either direction can have long-term repercussions: someone who spends high school cutting class and smoking dope might enjoy the moment but will likely pay a price later in life; someone who regularly turns down party invitations to pound the AP calculus study guide may, as an adult, mourn their wasted youth.

Seen in this light, youth sports are incredibly expensive. The dollar cost of soccer balls, hockey sticks, field time, gas used driving to games, and so on can certainly add up, but it pales next to the cost of time not spent doing something else. Every afternoon a kid spends at soccer practice is an afternoon not spent studying—an activity that could pay off more directly in getting into a better school, earning more money as an adult, and being able to afford a bigger house and his own kids' education. On the other hand, by studying, he would be giving up the chance to play soccer—which would let him have fun, develop life skills, and get some exercise. Even boiling the problem down to those two choices ignores all the other forgone options: he could learn the piano, get valuable sleep to help him grow and stay healthy, or just enjoy playing with Legos or watching *SpongeBob*. So youth sports, like most other childhood pastimes, are very expensive in "opportunity cost"—the alternative experiences a kid could have during the few precious years he has to both enjoy childhood and invest in his future.

You might think that economists can just do some sort of clever study to determine whether playing sports (organized or otherwise) as a child leads to adult success in the labor market. But it's not that easy. The ideal way to determine whether youth sports pay off in the labor market would be to randomly assign one bunch of kids to play sports and to bar another randomly chosen group from ever playing them. Then, when the kids had grown up, the study could look at the incomes of both groups and see which made more money. If the study found that adults who had played sports as kids made more, everyone could say confidently that investing in youth sports yields a financial return. But although randomized experiments are becoming much more common in the social sciences, nobody has ever done one on youth sports, and I doubt anyone ever will. Economists have been able to do conclusive studies about, for example, the effects of more education, growing up in an affluent neighborhood, and other factors, but they have not found credible "natural experiments" for youth sports participation.

Still, economists have done the best they can with the data they have. Several studies have shown that people who play more sports as kids make more money as adults. One study used a sample of Americans in their twenties. Those who had participated in organized sports in high school made 6 percent more, on average, holding other factors constant.[1] A recent study of German youths also showed that those who play youth sports obtain better wages and labor-market outcomes.[2] But even though these results are intriguing, we have to remember the mantra of introductory statistics class: correlation does not equal causation. Although the economists who conducted these studies made every effort to control for other factors, they could not clearly separate correlation from causation. Plausible alternative explanations exist that would not suggest that playing sports as a kid helps your career when you grow up.

For example, the thrill of victory we got from David's home run is not limited to Little League games; David and I are both competitive people. We measure success in wins and losses when we do pretty much anything. Watching *Jeopardy!* is a spirited event in our living room, with score carefully kept and many shouts of "I said it first!" We also both played a lot of youth sports. But organized sports did not make us competitive people; we already were that way. Perhaps a competitive nature, which can't be measured in the economists' analysis, is behind both success in the labor market and interest in youth sports programs. The researchers would not be able to identify competitiveness as the cause of the results.

The studies that have been done lead to the conclusion that playing sports as a kid may bring some benefit later in life. Every study found a correlation between increased youth sports activity and higher adult wages. But the effect, if it exists, is small. One recent study looked at data on American youth sports participation and, consistent with prior work, found that kids who play sports get more education, get paid more later in life, and are healthier. But the economists also concluded that these relationships are almost entirely because kids who participate in sports are different from kids who don't and that child athletes would be more successful and healthier whether they played sports or not.[3] If all that mattered was success in the labor market later in life, studying might have been a better use of time than long sports practices.

The implications for parents are pretty straightforward. The vast majority of kids have little or nothing to gain in the future from playing sports. As an investment, playing sports is hard to justify—if your kids don't like sports, don't force them into it. But for many kids, youth sports offer a great deal of simple consumption value. Kids really love to play sports, and since you only get to be a kid once, there is good reason to let them do so. The economist's bottom-line advice is simple: let your kid be a kid and play sports if she wants to.

Sports and College: A Very American Institution

If sports have any investment value for American kids, it can be summed up in one word: college. College can make youth sports pay off financially in four main ways.

The first and most direct payoff comes for a hypergifted kid who becomes a star athlete in college and then a professional. This consideration is not relevant for the vast majority of people.

The second possible reason was captured well in a *New York Times* feature about Matt Skoglund, whose experience might lead you to think that college can make youth sports pay off even if you never make a nickel as an athlete. Skoglund spent almost ten years as an attorney for the Natural Resources Defense Council directing its Northern Rockies operations out of his office in Bozeman, Montana.[4] He didn't make the kind of money many big-city lawyers make, but he took his compensation in lifestyle and working at his dream job for a cause he believes in. It was hockey that made this life possible. Maybe.

When he was in high school, Skoglund was the focus of a *New York Times* article on the value of sports for college admissions.[5] A native of the Chicago suburbs, Skoglund was a senior at Choate Rosemary Hall, a prestigious boarding school in Connecticut. His middling SAT scores were well below average for people admitted to Middlebury College, but the Middlebury hockey coach put Skoglund on his wish list. According to Skoglund, "Being a hockey player gave me access to a first-rate education." Research backs him on this. One study suggests that prestigious college admissions committees give an advantage to recruited athletes equivalent to an extra two hundred points on the SAT.[6]

So Skoglund went to the more prestigious Middlebury instead of, say, the University of Vermont or Lake Forest College.[7] From there, he was admitted to the University of Illinois law school and went on to a clerkship and two years as a litigator at a top Chicago firm before heading to the Rockies. If he had gone to one of those other schools, he might have ended up at a low-ranked law school and a less prestigious clerkship. The dream job might have been out of reach.

Or would it? Nobody knows. We can never know the alternative path Skoglund's life would have taken had he gone to one of those other schools. The "correlation is not causation" critique applies to Skoglund just as it did to the studies of youth sports discussed earlier. Hockey helped him attend a better college, but research is inconclusive about whether or not going to a better undergraduate school has long-term positive benefits. People who go to Harvard do better in the labor market, on average, than those who go to the University of Massachusetts, but Harvard admits people who are already on a faster track to success. We can't tease out Harvard's contributions from the personal attributes its students brought with them.

The third way the youth sports–college combination can pay off financially is through college scholarships.[8] In 2019–2020, approximately $4.2 billion of college scholarships were awarded to approximately 200,000 college athletes, an average of a little over $20,000 each. This means that about 1 percent of American students receive at least partial athletic scholarships. (Nearly 400,000 college athletes get no scholarship help.)[9]

College scholarships can be a huge benefit to some kids. But investing in a child's athletic endeavors just for the scholarship money probably isn't worth it. First, given that so few students get scholarships, and that most who do get only partial scholarships, the expected value for any one aspiring athlete is small. Second, the financial returns to a college education are huge. For a typical kid, paying the cost of college is a great investment that pays off. The savings from a scholarship are small compared to the benefits of the education itself.

None of these first three options provides an especially persuasive rationale for investing in youth sports, leaving just one way youth sports can pay off: they provide a set of skills that, together with a college education, lead to greater earnings later in life. We can certainly find examples to support this idea; Stanford's football team, for instance, has a program to hook players up with Silicon Valley firms and other employers, and the pipeline from top college lacrosse programs to Wall Street is so strong that one article claimed "having lacrosse on a résumé is a major advantage to grads entering the world of finance."[10] The logic comes down to some combination of two factors. First, sports provide a network of teammates, competitors, and fans who promote one another's careers. Second, the discipline that makes someone a star running back or lacrosse defender also makes that person a great consultant or trader.

If it seems plausible that sports and college might mix in a way that makes people more money later in life, and if plenty of anecdotes support the idea, does that mean you should encourage your kids to play sports in anticipation of financial benefits later?

One thing is clear: if playing sports gets kids to stay in school and makes them more likely to go to college, then youth sports can be justified solely on financial grounds. As I noted, it is well established that more education leads to higher income. One study showed that low-income teenagers who can commute to college, sparing them the cost of housing, fare better than comparable low-income teenagers who live far from a college and cannot afford higher education. Another study showed that sets of identical twins with different levels of education earned incomes that correlated with how much school they attended. A third study sampled students in states that allow teenagers to drop out of high school at a fixed age and showed that people whose birthdays forced them to stay in school an additional year earned more money, on average, than their counterparts who were able to skip the extra year.[11] Plenty of other cleverly designed studies, covering many countries and eras, have yielded the same results. Skeptics can certainly brainstorm confounding factors for any given study, but the evidence makes it clear that more education *causes* higher salaries.

The bottom line is that youth sports probably help a small but nontrivial set of American kids get more and better education than they otherwise would have, and this education pays off later in life. If hockey led Matt Skoglund to get more years of schooling than he would otherwise have gotten (for example, if hockey allowed him to get into Middlebury, and going to Middlebury led him to go to law school), then hockey improved his career path.

What If Your Kid Is Kevin Durant?

Living near Palo Alto, I see lots of parents who encourage their kids to play sports with no illusion that those kids will someday earn livings as pro athletes. These parents focus on their kids' formal education, for two primary reasons. First, the kids come from backgrounds that put them in a good position to do well at top American universities and quite possibly continue on to graduate school. These parents have every reason to think their kids are on track to the good life that goes with education: relatively high income, low risk of unemployment, better-than-average health, and other benefits. Second, while many of these kids are good athletes, few have the natural talents required to excel in professional sports. Some "option value" exists that any given kid will take his or her mediocre athletic genes and develop into a skilled athlete. But at some point, usually before a kid reaches high school, it becomes pretty clear to everyone (though the kid may take longer to catch on) that he or she will never run, jump, throw, or kick like LeBron James, Lionel Messi, or Serena Williams. Privileged kids from the suburbs generally play sports for fun, memories, and (maybe) the benefits of socialization and discipline.

But what if your kid is Kevin Durant? A working-class kid born in Washington, D.C., in 1988, Durant had a childhood very different from that of a Palo Alto Little Leaguer. His mother, Wanda Pratt, was relatively educated (she eventually earned a B.S. from Strayer University), but shortly after Durant was born, she became a single mother of two kids. Durant was raised by his mother and grandmother, and although they did not live in abject poverty, he did not grow up with many creature comforts or professional career opportunities.[12]

Durant's youth was focused on basketball—surely at some cost to his schooling. Obviously those investments paid off, as Durant now earns approximately $75 million per year in NBA salary and endorsements. But can parents of a kid like Durant justify the decision to expend resources on the kid's basketball future? Clearly the investments Durant and his family made look like great decisions in retrospect. But were they wise at the time?

For Durant, the two main reasons the typical Palo Alto kid should *not* focus on preparing for a sports career did not apply. First, coming from an underprivileged background and also, as a Black man, facing a labor market marked by systemic racism and historical discrimination, Durant's career prospects outside basketball were not promising. Fewer than 20 percent of African Americans graduate from college.[13] A Black man of working age who holds a full-time job earns an average of about $43,000 per year (half of what a typical college graduate earns), but only about 60 percent of Black men work full-time. The other 40 percent earn much less or zero. Coming from a family with modest resources further eclipsed Durant's labor-market prospects, as economic research shows that economic mobility to a better standard of living is slow in the United States, and much slower for African Americans. One recent study found that Black Americans "have substantially lower rates of upward mobility . . . than whites, leading to persistent disparities across generations."[14] Thus, in the society into which he was born, Durant's family might have rationally anticipated that basketball would be a higher-value play for him than it would be for a white family that was financially comfortable. Second, and even more important, Durant showed athletic promise and was unusually tall from a very young age.

Even so, Durant and his family had to decide that he would invest in basketball, and this investment surely came at some cost to his schooling. His godfather recalled asking, "Kevin, is this something you seriously want to do? OK, we're going to have to put in a lot of work." He made Durant go to daily training sessions and read basketball books, and also made him "write the six steps to a jump shot 500 times." He added, "But mostly, there were drills."[15]

As early as his junior year of high school, Durant reached a height of six feet eight inches.[16] That alone changes the odds of earning a living playing basketball. His height guaranteed he would be at least four standard deviations above the average height of an American man (he eventually reached six feet ten inches). That makes Durant taller than more than 99.99 percent of men: a man of his height is one in more than ten thousand.

Let's do some math to see what Durant's chances were. When Durant was in high school, approximately 320,000 African American boys who were born in 1988 lived in the United States. Of these, the numbers suggest that approximately forty-five would ever reach the height of six feet eight inches (Durant's height at the time, which is also the average height of players in the NBA).[17] Though he and his family could not have known this when he was in high school, a total of fifty Black men born in 1988 eventually played at least some minutes in the NBA. Twenty-one of these players had guaranteed contracts for the 2015–2016 season—the peak of their careers. Eight of them were at least six feet eight inches tall. Given that eight out of about forty-five Black men born in 1988 who were that tall had large NBA contracts, others spent time in the NBA, and still others made a healthy living playing basketball overseas, the odds that an athletic, hardworking kid as tall as Durant could earn a living playing basketball start to look pretty good.

Note, however, that this calculation changes dramatically as soon as an NBA wannabe concludes he will never be taller than about six feet. Almost no NBA players are that short, and given that lots of people are around six feet tall, the fraction of them who reach the NBA is essentially zero.

Another important caveat is that although Durant came from a humble background, one can't be sure his nonbasketball opportunities would have been limited to the low income that his demographics suggested. Given how hard he worked to develop his basketball skills, it seems safe to conclude that he has an unusual work ethic that could have paid off in other fields. Moreover, he is clearly very intelligent, and he is interested in education—although he left the University of Texas after his freshman season, when he was the second pick in the NBA draft, he continued to work toward a degree in the off-season.[18] Thus, it's possible that he could have gotten a good education and had a successful career in another field, although his chances of earning as much as he has earned from basketball were roughly zero. But even if he did not expect the riches he has achieved, for a six-foot-eight kid with limited family circumstances, investing time and effort in basketball seems like a pretty reasonable risk.

If we expand our view to include all of Durant's birth cohort, of the roughly 320,000 Black males born in 1988, almost 300 played in the NBA or the NFL at some point, and just under 200 were on an NBA or NFL roster in the fall of 2015. (I am focusing on that year because complete information for both athletes and the general U.S.

population is available for research.) The odds that a kid from this cohort grew up to be a pro are slight (about one in a thousand), but not multimillion-dollar-lottery slight. When we focus only on those who show signs of talent in high school—the point at which a focus on sports begins to be more costly—the odds look much more reasonable.

What are the returns for success? As you might imagine, they are substantial.[19] In 2015, the median income of an African American male born in 1988 was about $15,600, and the average was a little over $20,000. For the 2015 NFL season and the 2015–2016 NBA season, 184 African Americans born in 1988 spent some time on a team's roster, earning a total of $410 million in salary. This figure does not include endorsements, but it also does not deduct the agents' share of this income (3 to 4 percent in the NFL and NBA). These calculations lead to some startling conclusions:

1. *Between 6 and 7 percent of all the money earned by American Black men born in 1988 was earned by NFL and NBA players.* This suggests that the top 0.1 percent of the income distribution for this specific group earns approximately the same share of the group's total income as the top 0.1 percent of all Americans earn as a share of the total income in America.[20]

2. Including his endorsement income, *Kevin Durant's annual income represented almost 1 percent of all the money earned* by the more than 300,000 African American men born in 1988.

3. The incomes of the NFL stars Gerald McCoy and LeSean McCoy (no relation) each represented approximately 0.5 percent of the total income of African American men born in 1988.

I focused on men who were twenty-seven to twenty-eight years old because they were old enough to have signed large contracts but few had reached retirement age. I found no evidence of any other Black men born in 1988 who earned eight-figure incomes.[21]

Although the data clearly show that investing in sports makes sense for a small set of athletically gifted (and large) kids from difficult backgrounds, it's important to note that Durant was a perfect storm in terms of height and lack of alternatives to basketball. Two other Black men born in 1988 reached elite NBA status despite not standing out quite as much on one or both of these dimensions.

Russell Westbrook came from as humble a background as Durant's. Westbrook's father instilled a love of basketball in young Russell, who devoted a great deal of time to developing his skills. But at the point in his high school career where colleges start recruiting players, Westbrook was well under six feet tall and not an especially accurate shooter. His father advised Russell to "outwork them."[22] This strategy paid off: Westbrook grew to six feet three inches (big enough, though still small by NBA standards) and became a great player on all dimensions. But even though his father's advice paid off handsomely, it is quite possible that for the average kid who fit Westbrook's profile at age fifteen, the better advice would be to outwork his peers in the classroom rather than on the court.

Steph Curry was also late to grow into his eventual six-foot-three-inch frame, remaining short and scrawny well into college. But, unlike Westbrook and Durant, Curry—the son of the former NBA player Dell Curry—was raised in a well-to-do household. The economist Seth Stephens-Davidowitz has shown that, among NBA players, African Americans from relatively wealthy neighborhoods (like Curry) are overrepresented.[23] Although plenty of NBA players like Durant and Westbrook became superstars despite growing up with limited resources, many others, like Curry, had affluent childhoods. Unattractive opportunities outside sports are a good reason for kids like Durant to focus on sports, but they face the reality that kids from wealthier backgrounds are more likely to have professional coaches and good equipment.

Kevin Durant's family made a good decision to invest in basketball on his behalf, and the Palo Alto parents made a good decision to invest more in their kids' formal education. The question is, Where do you draw the line? Who else can justify going all out to invest in a life in sports?

It's actually very hard to come up with another group that combines the two key features highlighted earlier—high probability of success as a pro athlete and unattractive career prospects in other fields—as well as men from humble backgrounds who are extremely tall or (focusing on the NFL prospects) extremely large and muscular or extremely fast and dexterous.

Tall Black women are heavily overrepresented in the WNBA as well, but the financial value of WNBA success is meager compared to success in the men's game. Whereas Kevin Durant earns almost 1 percent of all the money earned by American Black men born in 1988, no WNBA player earns even 0.01 percent of the money earned by women of her race in her birth year.

Dominican baseball players are heavily overrepresented in Major League Baseball, and soccer players from Senegal are overrepresented in the French Ligue 1 (soccer). These people certainly have limited financial prospects in their own countries. But unlike predicting future NFL and NBA stars, telling who will become great is much harder when these players are young. Outliers based on physical size do not have such a clear advantage in baseball or soccer, and few kids who seem like superstars in their communities will ever receive a paycheck (or even a college scholarship) for playing their sport.

Sadly, not everyone understands the low probability of success. Some parents get blinded by dreams of their kids' stardom. A *New York Times Magazine* article described how one affluent Chinese family moved across the country to a premier golf training facility, where their three-year-old son, Xie Chengfeng, began to practice ceaselessly with the help and encouragement of his parents, plus coaches, tutors, and other adults whose attention had been acquired for the right price. Xie's case isn't an isolated one: in small but growing numbers, wealthy Chinese families are betting incredible sums of money and time that their children will someday make millions on the PGA Tour.[24]

Xie's family's investment in his golf future may be extreme, but many kids around the world, including the shortstops of Santo Domingo, the soccer players in Dakar, and girls playing tennis in Russia and Serbia, share similar dreams. Most of them will look back as adults and wish they had spent more time preparing for a more conventional life, but a few (maybe even Xie, who subsequently moved to Southern California and has done very well on the junior golf circuit) will reach their goals and inspire the next generation to spend their childhood years trying to become superstars.

2

What Do Silicon Valley and Czech Women's Tennis Have in Common?

Liechtenstein, a tiny principality between Switzerland and Austria with just thirty-seven thousand inhabitants spread across sixty-two square miles, is disproportionately blessed. For starters, the lure of its low corporate tax rate has given it the highest gross domestic product (GDP) per capita of any country in the world. Even better, Liechtenstein has no standing army, so its taxpayers get to keep more of that wealth than citizens of larger countries, which tend to spend substantially on their militaries. And somehow, minuscule Liechtenstein manages to be the world's leading manufacturer of false teeth.

Of more interest to us, however, is that Liechtenstein is home to Tina Weirather, a skier who was a fixture on the World Cup circuit in both the downhill and super G events throughout the 2010s. Weirather, whose Austrian mother and Liechtensteiner father were both World Cup skiers, was internationally competitive from an early age. She moved in and out of the top ten in the women's Alpine skiing world rankings and took home the bronze medal in the super G in the 2018 Winter Olympics. Despite being her home country's only athlete of international caliber during her career, she made Liechtenstein, on a per capita basis, the greatest sports powerhouse in the world.

Liechtenstein's statistical dominance of global athletics is well documented, if you know where to look. The country places first on the list of all-time Olympic medal-winning countries per capita; its nine medals, all in Alpine skiing, give Liechtenstein about three times more medals per capita than the second-place country, Norway. China and the United States churn out hundreds of athletic super-stars across dozens of disciplines: China has earned 0.449 Olympic medals per million inhabitants, while the United States fares much better at 9.02. But that output pales in comparison to Liechtenstein's 274 medals per million.[1] The disparity points to just how unprece-dented it is for a group of thirty-seven thousand people to consis-tently produce one or two world-beating skiers every decade or so. But Liechtenstein has a natural advantage that is far more helpful to its skiers than low tax rates, demilitarization, or even false teeth: the entire country has easy access to snow and mountains.

Given this geography, it makes sense that Liechtenstein can boast such high rates of athletic success. Liechtenstein is one of several countries to channel either natural resources or strategic investment—or both—into an advantage in a single sport, as the dominance of Norwegian cross-country skiers, American basketball players, and East African marathoners makes clear.

Measuring Geographic Dominance

Stories about a country dominating a single sport are interesting, but I wanted to be a bit more systematic and quantitative in assessing dynasties. With that in mind, I developed a standardized measure of national athletic dominance to allow for reasonable comparisons across countries and sports. The Population-Adjusted Power Index, or PAPI, tells us a country's strength in a given sport relative to its population. To measure PAPI, I tracked down the top 25 rankings in sixteen individual sports that have international men's and women's sports associations.[2] Then I counted the nationalities of the members of the top 25 on each of the 32 circuits. Finally, I found the ratio between a country's representation in a given top 25 and its overall population.

Consider a few groups with high scores. In my data set, Romania has one of the world's top 25 women's skeleton racers; Poland has two top 25 men's kayakers; and the United States has 16 of the world's top 25 men's golfers. The three countries' shares of the world population, from smallest to largest, are 0.28 percent, 0.54 percent, and 4.44 percent. Dividing the first number (share of the top 25 in the given sport) by the second (share of world population) yields the countries' PAPI scores in their respective sports: all about 14.5. Romania's single top-25 skeleton racer gives it 14.5 times as many top-25 women's skeleton racers as it would have if its share of the world's top-25 skeleton racers matched its share of the world's population. Likewise, if top-25 men's golfers were distributed across countries in the same proportions as the world's population, the United States would have a little more than one. Its actual number, 16 of the top 25, is about 14.5 times its expected share.

Thus, although the raw numbers differ greatly, Romanian women's skeleton, Polish men's kayak, and American men's golf are all, by PAPI, at about the same strength. For comparison's sake, the top PAPI in my sample (Liechtenstein's women's Alpine skiers) is 7,718. Note that a PAPI of 1.0 means that a country has exactly the same share of top-25 athletes in a sport as its share of the world's population. For example, China has 5 of the top 25 male badminton players, and since it has about one-fifth of the world's population, China's PAPI in men's badminton is very close to 1. The vast majority of PAPIs are zero, given that most countries have zero athletes in any given top-25 ranking.

The Napa Valley of Scandinavia

The example of skiing in Liechtenstein is a classic case of "comparative advantage"—that is, it is easy for Liechtensteiners to be better at skiing because, compared with people almost everywhere else, they have easy access to mountains and snow. That doesn't mean Liechtenstein was guaranteed to be good at skiing; it could have limited resources for training or other constraints that would hold potential skiers back. But the country's advantage is "comparative" because, holding other things constant, it is *comparatively* easy for Liechtensteiners to be good skiers relative to being, for example, good badminton players, and relative to how easy it would be for a Costa Rican to become a good skier.

The idea of comparative advantage extends far beyond sports; it is a broad and important economic force that drives much of the geography of business. When asked to name the single most important insight in economics, a nontrivial number of academic economists will choose comparative advantage. Chilean copper, Vietnamese fish, Thai rice, and the wines of California, Australia, and New Zealand (all of which have climates ideally suited to grape growing) reflect the same economic phenomenon as Liechtensteiner skiers. Just as resources and climate make it sensible for Chile to mine copper and Thailand to grow rice (and then to use trade to make both countries better off), Liechtenstein produces more than its share of skiers, and the United States an abundance of golfers. Sports fans the world over are better off because they can watch top athletes who have come from the best breeding grounds.

Of course, Liechtenstein is not alone (or even unusual) in having a climate and topography favorable to skiing. Take its not-quite-neighbor Norway. Norway has plenty of snow and plenty of mountains, giving it a similar natural advantage in downhill skiing. But other countries, such as Liechtenstein, have their ski slopes far closer to population centers. In Norway, the mountains are relatively remote, and that distance is just one of several obstacles for aspiring Norwegian downhill skiers: Norway is far enough north that it gets limited daylight, a big problem for downhill skiers, and it is also extremely cold, which makes sitting in a chairlift pretty uncomfortable.

So although Norway has not abandoned downhill—in fact, the Norwegian downhill skiing program is fairly strong, with two men and one woman among the top 25 skiers—it has not focused on the sport to the same extent as countries like Liechtenstein. Rather, Norway has parlayed its challenges in downhill (compared with several other snowy countries) into strengths in Nordic, or cross-country, skiing. To practice effectively, cross-country skiers need less daylight than downhill skiers; they stay warm more easily because they are moving constantly; and they do not need access to mountains. Norwegian population centers tend to be close to wilderness (more so than, for example, those in Sweden), which makes it easy for Norwegians to practice cross-country skiing.[3] These characteristics make cross-country skiing a potential gold mine for the Norwegian athletic program.

And Norway has cashed in on this comparative advantage. Home to less than one-tenth of 1 percent of the world's population (and fewer people than Minnesota), Norway took home more than half of the gold medals and more than a third of all medals awarded for cross-country skiing at the 2018 Winter Olympics. Its men's and women's cross-country skiers attained the second- and third-highest PAPI scores, respectively, of all the national athletic programs I tracked: of the top 25 cross-country skiers worldwide, ten men and eight women were Norwegian, for respective PAPI scores of 561 and 449. That is, Norway has as many top-25 cross-country men skiers as we would expect, proportionally, from a country 561 times Norway's size. Norwegian cross-country skiers trail only Liechtenstein's women's skiers in the PAPI sample—in other words, they trail only Tina Weirather.

Although it isn't surprising that Norway is good at cross-country skiing, it's a little surprising that Norwegian skiers are so good, given that Russia, Finland, and Sweden have similar advantages. Even though each of those nations has multiple top-25 cross-country skiers, they don't come near Norway's dominance. Why? Because Norway has made strategic use of some complementary advantages.

As it happens, in addition to snow, Norway owns a bounty of another valuable resource: oil. Sustained exportation of that oil has allowed Norway to become nearly as wealthy as Liechtenstein on a per capita basis while maintaining a much larger (if still fairly small) population. At the same time, Norway's government is as socialistic as any in the developed world, so that the government controls much of the country's substantial wealth and can invest it strategically. One of the government's many social programs channels a hefty sum (by law, a minimum of about $300 million per year) into building youth athletic facilities and paying good wages to highly skilled coaches who identify and develop talented skiers from an early age.[4]

The Norwegian Confederation of Sports (NIF), the government agency that oversees Norway's Olympic committee and its broader investment in sports, manages 54 federations, 19 regional sports confederations, 366 local sports councils, and over 11,000 local sports clubs. These organizations are funded with the help of revenues from the national lottery.[5] Local sports clubs form the core of Norwegians' sports experiences when they are young, training them and identifying those who will move on to elite programs. Norway has six high schools known as the Norwegian College of Elite Sport, employing seventy-nine coaches recruited from around the world.[6] From there, many athletes move to full-time training centers. Although the earlier discussion of youth sports suggests that large investments are not

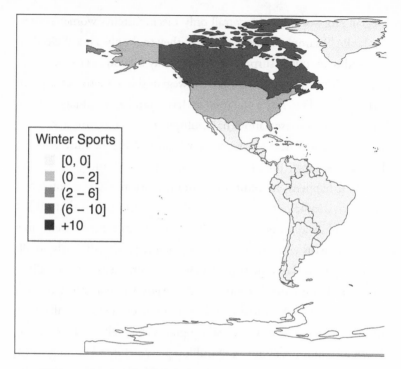

Figure 1. Average PAPI for Alpine skiing, Nordic skiing, and skeleton
(Illustration by Julio C. Franco)

necessarily a good idea for individuals, the country of Norway clearly believes they are valuable at a national level.

This financial and cultural investment gives Norway a big advantage over other countries in sports. But combining that investment with Norway's natural advantages makes it an unprecedented powerhouse. Plenty of countries have natural advantages in certain sports, but few exploit them as well as Norway does in cross-country skiing. In this sense, Norway is the Napa Valley of cross-country skiing. Napa Valley wineries have excellent natural conditions for growing grapes, and thanks to a surplus of Northern California millionaires looking for an expensive hobby, the wineries have the resources to turn those

grapes into world-class wines. Napa Valley wines and Norwegian cross-country skiers may not offer the best return on investment, but both combine their climate-based comparative advantage with a wealth of resources to become the best (or among the best) in the world.

The importance of comparative advantage can be shown graphically (figure 1). On this world map, the darkness of each country corresponds to the average PAPI in three sports where wintry conditions confer a large advantage: Alpine (downhill) skiing, Nordic (cross-country) skiing, and skeleton. Virtually all the darkness is above the fiftieth parallel, and PAPIs are basically zero for any country not well above the equator.

The same map can be used to diagram all sixteen of the sports in the PAPI sample (figure 2). The Nordic countries and Canada still do

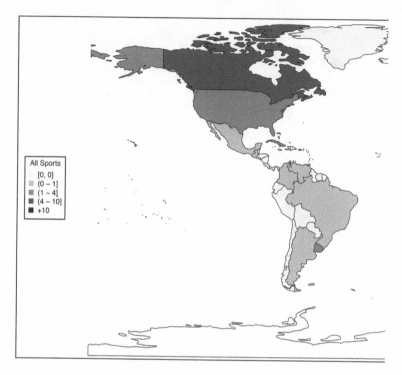

Figure 2. Average PAPI for sixteen individual sports
(Illustration by Julio C. Franco)

very well by this broader measure, but the rest of the world does much better. The two figures together bring out the importance of comparative advantage; the Nordic countries and Canada are excellent at sports in general, but they are particularly excellent at winter sports.

When Running Marathons Is the Best Option

Far away from Norway is the most dominant group in any sport: East African marathoners. Although Norwegian cross-country skiers are a story of comparative advantage enhanced by plentiful complementary resources (that is, oil money), East African marathoners are

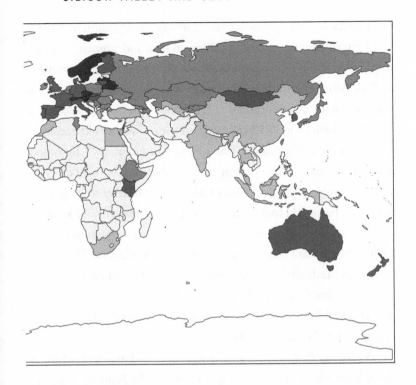

a story of geographic comparative advantage enhanced by *lack* of complementary resources.

Their dominance is truly absolute. A while back, when I first looked up the top 25 male marathoners, the Italian runner Daniele Meucci was the sole representative of any country not named Ethiopia or Kenya. Meucci ranked twenty-fifth. The top 24 male marathon runners in the world all came from Ethiopia or Kenya. When I checked back a few months later, Meucci had slipped, and the highest-ranked marathoner not from East Africa was tied for forty-fifth with two Kenyans. Female marathoners from East Africa are dominant by any metric other than comparison to their male counterparts: 20 of the top 25 women's marathoners come from Ethiopia and Kenya, including the top 12.[7]

Kenyan male marathoners rank a strong twenty-ninth in PAPI— and Kenyan women, as well as Ethiopian men and women, also have respectable scores—but PAPI does not do justice to the dominance of East African marathoners. Kenya, with 44 million people, and Ethiopia, with 94 million, both have populations large enough to eliminate them from PAPI competition with countries like Liechtenstein. A more apt measure is the Herfindahl index, used by economists to measure how concentrated an industry is. Unlike PAPI, which measures a single country's dominance relative to its population, the Herfindahl index measures concentration within a small set of countries. Among all sport-gender combinations, marathon has the highest Herfindahl index of all sports for both genders.[8] In fact, the marathon "industry" scored higher on the Herfindahl index than the beer or breakfast cereal industries, traditionally two of the most concentrated in the world. As cartels go, Kenyan and Ethiopian marathoners put OPEC to shame.

A statistic that assesses an entire country's dominance of marathon, however, does not do proper justice to the Kalenjin tribe and its close relatives, which together produce almost all East African runners. David Epstein, the author of a book about the science of athletes, told an interviewer: "There are 17 American men in history who have run under 2:10 in the marathon. There were 32 Kalenjin who did it in October of 2011."[9]

How can this small part of Africa dominate a sport so thoroughly? Social scientists, biological scientists, and sports pundits have long debated the question. To an economist, two factors appear to be critical: geographic advantage and a lack of alternatives.

First, parts of Kenya and the surrounding region provide a natural advantage to native runners similar to what Norwegians experience in cross-country skiing. Kalenjin live at high altitudes, which confers an advantage for effective and efficient practice of endurance sports. The local weather is conducive to an active life and being out-doors. Schools are often far away, so kids get used to walking (and, according to some reports, running barefoot) for long distances. Some scholars have argued that the local environment leads to a carbohydrate-heavy diet, which may help in endurance training.[10]

There is also a cultural explanation, arguably related to the natural environment. Many Kalenjin children go through an initiation ceremony that involves crawling through brush, getting beaten, and anesthesia-free circumcision. This and other cultural factors, some argue, condition Kalenjins to be able to run through pain. According to a report by NPR, "In traditional Kalenjin society, pushing through pain isn't only a desired trait, it's also part of what makes you a man or a woman."[11]

In addition to these natural advantages (speculative and other-wise), lack of resources motivates East African runners' development. For running, the equipment and land costs of training are trivial—unlike for sports like sailing or golf—so that even people from rela-tively low-income areas are not at a disadvantage. If Kenya's weather and altitude (especially in the areas where Kalenjin live) were condu-cive to developing skiers, then the locals, lacking the resources to pay for facilities, equipment, and specialized coaches, might not be able to take advantage. But even a poor country can afford to develop runners.

Motivation matters too. Norwegian cross-country coaches may find it difficult to get a Norwegian teenager to spend excessive amounts of time skiing when that kid is starting to worry about get-ting into college and eventually getting a good job. Rural East Afri-can children typically do not have bright career prospects and thus have strong incentives to become runners. Daniel Lieberman, a Har-vard biology professor who has studied East African runners, says he thinks the most important reason for their success is the region's widespread poverty and (as an economist might put it) the low opportunity cost of pursuing running. "There are almost no jobs apart from subsistence farmers," Lieberman says. The author Adharanand Finn adds, "In Kenya the life of an athlete is one of relative comfort. Eat, sleep and run. It beats digging the earth all day with a hand plough."[12]

If Norway is the Napa Valley of cross-country skiing—geographic advantage combined with plenty of resources—then East Africa is the Nauru of marathon running. Nauru, an island nation in the central Pacific, had large reserves of phosphates thanks to many centuries of built-up bird droppings. Early in the twentieth century, Nauru began to mine these deposits, which meant that the island was literally depleted. The residents of Nauru didn't particularly want to turn their island into a strip mine, but having few other economic opportunities, they went with their comparative advantage. Many Kenyan and Ethiopian runners, if they had better access to education and careers, would no doubt choose business, medicine, or another profession. But given that the most readily available alternative is subsistence farming, many find that the best option is to pursue running.

Martina Navratilova Is Hewlett. And Packard.

The Czech Republic is home to about ten million people. The country has cold winters and plenty of rainfall. It has no natural advantage relevant to producing tennis players. Yet Czech women's tennis ranks 25th in PAPI out of 356. There are enough Czech women in the top 25 to proportionately represent a country 108 times larger than the Czech Republic.

How did the Czech Republic become such a force in women's tennis without any comparative advantage? Simple: over decades, the country has developed a huge network of Czechs trying to become tennis players. As is usually the case when a network pops up in an environment that gives it no natural advantage, the growth was driven by historical circumstance. Back when the Czech Republic was part of the Austro-Hungarian Empire (and even before), the local nobility took to tennis. Competitive tennis in what is now the Czech Republic began in 1879, just two years after the first tournament at Wimbledon. Tennis, and sports generally, has always been culturally important among Czechs. There have always been plenty of great Czech tennis players of both genders, but the country's most gifted male athletes often gravitate to hockey or soccer. Although some Czech girls are drawn away by winter sports, at which Czechs also excel, it seems that a higher proportion of the most athletically talented dedicate themselves to tennis.

Thus, three factors have come together to make the Czech Republic a women's tennis powerhouse despite the lack of natural advantage: focus on the game through local clubs, parents, and coaches; investment and focus during the Soviet era; and Martina Navratilova.

Jan Kodes, a Czech tennis star who won three Grand Slam events in the early 1970s, described his country's success this way: "Our history goes back to 1893 with the first lawn tennis club. And there's the background of the small club. There's always somebody to tell you how to hold the racket and hit the ball. They may be unknown people, unknown coaches, who know more about the game than some top-name coaches."[13]

Hana Mandlikova, a four-time Grand Slam winner who was born in Prague, grew up in this system. Her father attributed her success, and the success of Czech tennis generally, to the quality of coaches, a focus on basic technique, and "fanatic parents" (including himself) who religiously took their children to far-flung tournaments run by the tennis federation. "Nowhere during my travels have I seen things for children so well organized as here," he told *Sports Illustrated*.[14] The

Czech legend Martina Navratilova has said that the club system and the early and constant competitions were responsible for later generations of Czech women's success, noting, "In these clubs, you hang out. . . . You become really competitive and learn the sport the way it should be taught, which is through competition."[15]

Navratilova's comment points to one thing that makes Czech girls so good at tennis: other Czech girls. Having a sport on which people focus, be it cross-country skiing, marathon running, or tennis, brings out kids' competitive spirit. Not only do they want to win, but they have a supply of friends and competitors against whom to hone their skills. Competition leads to innovation, as economists have long emphasized. Tougher competition makes athletes better just as it makes companies better. They have to find new ways to beat the competition. Czech girls learn to get better by playing each other, and they build on each other's improvements.

Much like the Norwegian government today, the Czech government in the Soviet era made large investments in these clubs and the tennis system. It also happily took credit for the players' achievements, writing that "the main cause of success is the support of the Czechoslovak Central Committee."[16] Clubs spread throughout the country, and talent scouts searched the elementary schools for potential champions as young as six. The most highly skilled players moved to a network of training centers, housed within existing clubs, where they were professionally coached, subjected to rigorous practice regimens, and given the best equipment. At any time, up to ninety thousand players played in the Czech club system and about sixty teenagers in the super-elite program.[17]

But a key reason why the Czech youth system turned out the current crop of top women's tennis players is Martina Navratilova. One of the all-time great female tennis players, Navratilova won 18 Grand Slam singles titles and another 41 between women's and mixed doubles. Her 59 total Grand Slam titles are second all-time to Australia's Margaret Court, and Navratilova's battles with the American player Chris Evert—now an ESPN commentator—elevated women's tennis to new heights of viewership and prize money. Navratilova inspired countless Czech girls to go down to the local tennis club and give it a try. As a result, the American numerical advantage was largely undone; there were a lot fewer Czech girls than American girls, but a large proportion of Czech girls play tennis, while the Americans play basketball, softball, or golf. A small country can have a big presence if the infrastructure for success exists and a large fraction of the population is drawn to the sport.

Petra Kvitova, who has won two Wimbledon championships and has been ranked as high as second in the world, is a typical example of the Czech tennis legacy's impact. She was born in Bilovec, a small town several hours from Prague. According to her website, "Her family spent a lot of time playing tennis at the local club," and her father "used to show Petra videos of Martina Navratilova playing at Wimbledon, which she would watch with fascination." Kvitova writes, "I have so much respect for Martina, I watched her on television when I was a child, and that's where I learnt about Wimbledon and playing on grass."[18] Kvitova showed great promise and at age sixteen moved to a full-time tennis school (the club system and elite schools outlived the Soviet era). After becoming a successful pro, Kvitova paid homage to Navratilova in a series called "My Hero" for *Tennis* magazine.[19]

To get a better sense of Czech tennis players' geographic dominance in the absence of any natural advantage, think of the clustering of major technology companies in Silicon Valley. Like the early Czech competitive tennis leagues, Stanford University developed a strength in technical and business education, creating a steady supply of both new companies and technical talent to staff them; like the Czech leagues, Stanford's presence provided infrastructure in a relatively narrow field in a relatively small region. In 1939, two Stanford graduates, William Hewlett and David Packard, founded a company in Palo Alto, and the growth of Hewlett-Packard and the network of technology companies that started up in the surrounding area made Silicon Valley what it is today. Hewlett and Packard did for Silicon Valley what Martina Navratilova did for Czech women's tennis: they took an existing infrastructure and started a self-sustaining network around it. In both cases, no natural advantage existed (they don't actually mine silicon in Silicon Valley; the industry could just as easily have developed in Seattle or Saint Louis), but that didn't stop the region from becoming dominant in the field.

An Improbably Dominant Dynasty

If Norway's cross-country ski dominance shows how natural advantage can fuse with complementary economic factors to create a niche, and the Czech Republic's success in women's tennis shows how happenstance and investments can do the same, then South Korea's unprecedented emergence in a seemingly random sport falls somewhere in between. South Korean women do not dominate golf to quite the degree that East Africans dominate marathons, but they are perhaps the most improbable persistent sports dynasty of all.

South Korea has more than 1,300 people per square mile, making it the fourteenth-densest country in the world (and third, behind Bangladesh and Taiwan, if you ignore microscopic countries like Vatican City and Barbados); such urban cramming leaves little space for athletic facilities. South Korea also has few natural resources beyond a handful of mines in the northern part of the country. It has no obvious advantage in either sports or economics.

Still, South Korea has become a rich country and has managed to find success in an array of sports, from archery to modern pentathlon to judo. Over the last few decades, South Korea has placed in the top ten medal winners at most Olympic Games, both summer and winter. But its Olympic success is dwarfed by its dominance of one sport: over a twenty-three-year period starting with the first Korean woman ever to win a golf major tournament, twenty different Korean women have won thirty-four major golf titles (and three more were won by women who were Korean citizens at birth). In a recent nine-year run, South Koreans claimed twenty-two of the forty-three (yes, more than half) major championship titles in LPGA golf.

Granted, South Korean women's golfers rank a pedestrian fifty-third in PAPI. PAPI is weighted toward countries with very small populations that can produce a few elite athletes in one sport. Even so, the South Korean women's golf PAPI of 62 is impressive—the country has as many top-25 golfers as we would expect from a country 62 times its size. Their PAPI, which ranks second among countries with at least 15 million inhabitants—behind Kenyan male marathoners—is particularly impressive given the country's rapid ascension from nonentity in the sport to powerhouse. This seemingly unnatural phenomenon is explained in large part by a unique collection of economic and cultural conditions that primed South Korea for a women's golf boom.

First, South Korean children are believed to be the most focused and overworked in the developed world. Perhaps not coincidentally, they are also the most miserable. An international survey by the Paris-based Organisation for Economic Co-operation and Development (OECD) placed Korea dead last in its assessment of children's happiness in school. Of all the countries surveyed, Korean parents had the highest expectations that their children would graduate from college, but the lowest rate of eating dinner with their children.[20] Every November, graduating South Korean high school students take the CSAT, an aptitude test that largely determines college placement. Results are considered so important that, on testing day, the stock market opens late so that parents can support test takers before going to work, and flights are canceled to avoid noise distractions. Students who under-perform their CSAT expectations have a significantly increased risk of suicide. South Korea, more broadly, has the highest suicide rate of any OECD country by far.[21]

Gender inequality is also dramatic in South Korea. The country placed 108th out of 153 countries sampled in the World Economic Forum's Global Gender Gap Report, beating only Turkey among de-veloped nations. *The Economist* gives an even harsher evaluation, plac-ing South Korea dead last among twenty-nine countries in its glass-ceiling index. Though South Korea elected a female president in 2013, Korean women occupy senior jobs at astonishingly low rates overall.[22]

On a more positive note, Korea historically has one of the high-est savings rates in the world. Of thirty OECD countries, its savings rate was recently second highest (to Norway), and it has been at or near the top of this ranking for decades.[23] This consistent standing likely reflects a cultural inclination to forgo gratification today for security tomorrow.

Korea thus offers an interesting set of extremes: significant wealth and high savings alongside unhappy children and staggering gender inequality. This combination of attributes, it turns out, may be ideal for breeding world-class female golfers. Nothing increases one's like-lihood of becoming a pro athlete like consistent, intense work, which is expected of Korean children in any field. But in Korea, girls get substantially less out of an investment in school than boys do: the 37 percent pay gap between genders provides less incentive for girls to push themselves academically.[24] For Korean girls, then, taking time away from schoolwork to practice a sport might seem like a good investment. Korean boys have reason to study hard and acquire the skills that will help them in the professional marketplace; girls have more incentive to forgo that study and do something else, like practice golf.

This reasoning is borne out empirically by the country's lack of similar success in men's golf. Korean men's golfing glory is limited to Y. E. Yang's anomalous PGA Championship title in 2009—he was ranked 110th in the world at the time and quickly returned to obscurity—and veteran pro K. J. Choi's decent but unspectacular career. Recently, the highest-ranked Korean man was eighteenth in the world, and the country had four of the top one hundred men's golfers. At the same time, a Korean woman (Jin-Young Ko) was number one in the world; 5 of the top 10 women golfers and 36 of the top 100 were Korean.[25] To be fair, another factor contributing to the gender disparity in golf performance is Korea's two-year military service requirement for men, but this likely isn't the sole barrier. Choi, for instance, worked as a sentry for the army during the day and practiced golf at night.

But why golf? Well, for one thing, it's not just golf. South Korean women have high PAPIs, for example, in archery (with seven of the world's top 25 archers) and short-track speed skating (with four of the top 10). If you look carefully, you can see that Korea is quite dark in figure 2's summary of PAPIs across sports, mainly thanks to its women athletes. But Korea's strength in golf may be partially due to the success of Korean golfer Se Ri Pak. Much like the Czech tennis star Martina Navratilova, Pak was a trailblazer in the Korean women's golf world. Her win at the U.S. Women's Open in 1998 was the first major championship for a Korean golfer. Although she was less of a pioneer than Navratilova—other Korean major champions were well on their way to golf success before Pak's breakthrough—her success functioned in a similar way. Many of today's Korean golf stars cite Pak as an inspiration. For example, So Yeon Ryu, a former U.S. Women's Open champion, said, "After Se Ri won the U.S. Women's Open, I really got interested in golf."[26] Seven-time major champion Inbee Park said that her parents took her to the driving range for the first time right after Se Ri Pak's first major victory.[27]

In the case of South Korea, then, preexisting economic circumstances created the potential for geographic success, which was catalyzed by the success of Se Ri Pak. Together, these conditions likely helped take the nation's women's golf elite to the next level of dominance.

Sometimes an area becomes dominant through natural advantages: Norwegian cross-country skiers, Napa Valley wineries. But some titans of sports and industry simply come from the right alignment of stars. Coincidences happen and even have long-term consequences. South Korean women dominate golf because of savings, gender discrimination, and a pioneer. Czech women punch above their weight in tennis because of the tastes of rich people a few hundred years ago and the success of one woman forty years ago. A small peninsula in Northern California evolved from the world's largest apricot grower into the world's leading high-tech region because one local university produced students who opened some computer and semiconductor firms there.

Once these dynasties become established through some combination of luck and coincidence, they become hard to topple. I would bet that Czech women tennis players and South Korean women golfers will still be dominant ten years from now because advantages, both in sports and in the economy, tend to persist. For example, the United States has enjoyed a perennial advantage in world basketball competition in the same way that Silicon Valley now has a huge lead in technology. Other countries have developed their basketball programs and made some progress relative to Team USA, just as technology clusters in Austin (Texas), Skolkovo (outside Moscow), and Tel Aviv (Israel) have made strides relative to Silicon Valley. Still, the big leads and reinforcing network effects of Team USA basketball and Silicon Valley—and Czech women's tennis—will take decades to match.

3

Why Do Athletes Cheat and Lie?

In the summer of 1998, Mark McGwire and Sammy Sosa were living legends. Hot in pursuit of Roger Maris's single-season home run record, the two sluggers traded long bomb after long bomb as the year wore on and Maris's sixty-one-homer mark grew closer. The story helped to rejuvenate baseball in the wake of its crippling strike in 1994: two media-friendly stars, each quick to heap praise on the other, were chasing one of the sport's most storied records. The pinnacle of the months-long spectacle came on September 8, when McGwire, playing for the Saint Louis Cardinals, hit his record-breaking sixty-second home run against Sosa's Chicago Cubs. As McGwire rounded the bases, Sosa famously jogged in from the outfield to congratulate him at home plate, a lasting image of sportsmanship and respect that was hailed as an encapsulation of everything good about baseball. McGwire ended the year with seventy home runs, Sosa with sixty-six, and both were immortalized for their roles in one of the most exciting baseball seasons ever.

The next time McGwire and Sosa made headlines together was in March 2005. This time, the venue was not the friendly confines of Wrigley Field in Chicago but the august halls of the U.S. Capitol, where they were testifying at a congressional hearing. As two of the most prominent baseball stars of recent years, they had been called before the House of Representatives Committee on Government Reform to testify about growing concerns over the use of performance-enhancing drugs in baseball. Neither man, it turned out, had much to say. McGwire repeatedly told the congressional committee, "I'm not here to talk about the past," while Sosa claimed that he did not speak English well enough to testify and issued a terse statement through his interpreter that he had never used steroids.[1]

The congressional hearing only marked the beginning of baseball's internal war on drugs. On December 13, 2007, with some fanfare, former senator George Mitchell issued his commissioned report on the steroid problem. At the end of the report's four-hundred-odd pages, he included among his findings and recommendations the following lament: "The players who follow the law and the rules . . . are faced with the painful choice of either being placed at a competitive disadvantage or becoming illegal users themselves. No one should have to make that choice."

Here Mitchell hit the nail on the head. A number of factors presumably go into deciding whether or not to take steroids—including health concerns, religious beliefs, and willingness to lie—but one consideration clearly at or near the top of the list is how these drugs will affect the athlete's performance relative to his peers. If McGwire was on steroids and Sosa wanted to keep pace, he would probably have had to take them too—and vice versa.

In economics terms, McGwire and Sosa faced a "prisoner's dilemma," a situation that can turn otherwise reasonable people into drug users, cheaters, and liars.

Can a Clean Cyclist Win the Tour de France?

Lance Armstrong, a seven-time Tour de France champion and winner of the Best Male Athlete ESPY and *Sports Illustrated* Sportsman of the Year awards, is no longer a popular man. He makes perennial appearances (sometimes at the top) on *Forbes*'s annual "most disliked athlete" list. Once sponsored by national brands such as Nike, Michelob Ultra, and 24 Hour Fitness, Armstrong now struggles to find even small bike companies willing to pay for his endorsement. His already-battered image suffered a knockout blow when he confessed his longtime use of banned substances to Oprah Winfrey on national television, confirming an unpleasant truth that was quickly becoming undeniable in the face of a mountain of evidence. The title of his best-selling book, *It's Not About the Bike,* took on an ironic new meaning when, for Armstrong, it became all about the doping.

But is Armstrong really such a bad guy? Or simply a victim of circumstance?

No economist would condone Armstrong's behavior, but plenty of economists would call it a predictable response to the incentives he faced. To see why, imagine you are a talented young cyclist who has been winning junior competitions for years. You're about to participate in your first Tour de France, excited to finally get your shot on the big stage. As soon as the race begins, however, you realize there's something different at this level. It's no surprise that all the athletes have intense workout regimens, tightly regulated diets, and cutting-edge equipment. But you quickly gather that they're also all using performance-enhancing drugs, something you've never been exposed to before. Should you give up and find a new career, or suck it up and start injecting yourself?

Some people would walk away. Cheating and lying about illegal drug use is a psychologically taxing behavior for most people, and those emotional costs might be so high that some athletes would walk away from a career in which success requires such consistent dishonesty. But for many others, the rational choice is easy in a different way. After years of investment in cycling, it seems only logical to start doping. If everyone is doing it, then you have no choice if you want to remain competitive. There are some ethical hang-ups, but cyclists certainly wouldn't be the first group of professionals to abandon their collective morals for the sake of their respective careers.

But how did this happen in the first place? How did the sport get to the point where all the top cyclists are alleged to be doping? When the Tour de France started in 1903, performance-enhancing drugs (PEDs) didn't exist, but that doesn't mean everyone rode clean. Ingesting substances has been a part of the Tour from the beginning. A top competitor was disqualified from the inaugural race for riding in the slipstream of a car, and nine riders were bounced the following year for taking cars and trains as shortcuts. They also used substances. One recent reporter, looking at the Tour's history, concluded, "From the earliest days of the race, entrants drank to deaden the monotony, huffed ether to tamp down the pain, took amphetamines for stamina, or opiates to ease aches and cramps." The 1923 winner told a reporter, "Cocaine to go in our eyes, chloroform for our gums, and do you want to see the pills?"[2]

Drugs were not banned until 1965, commencing an ongoing arms race in which riders seek new and innovative ways to cheat while Tour officials try (futilely, for the most part) to catch cheaters by means of more sophisticated testing. We can turn to the notorious prisoner's dilemma to get some insight into why riders cheat.

Suppose the police bring in two suspects who are believed to have jointly committed a robbery and place them in separate rooms. A detective goes into one room, then the other, and tells each prisoner that he has two choices: he can keep his mouth shut, which would incur a one-year sentence, or he can rat the other guy out, which would allow him to go free while the other guy serves a five-year sentence. The only catch? If both guys rat, they'll both be stuck with three-year sentences.

As you may know, the prisoner's dilemma has an elegant solution. Every prisoner, every time, should choose to rat. Whatever the other prisoner does, ratting is the better option: if the other guy keeps his mouth shut, the first guy goes free if he rats his partner out, but serves a year in jail if he too keeps his mouth shut. Meanwhile, if the other guy rats, the first guy can either rat too and take the three-year sentence, or keep his mouth shut and be stuck doing five years. The reason it's considered a dilemma is that the best *collective* choice is for both prisoners to keep quiet; then they serve a total of two years between them, versus a minimum of five years under all other options.[3]

Now consider a cyclist's dilemma. Let's start by making a few assumptions that probably approximate real-life conditions. First, let's say doping increases each cyclist's speed by enough that if he takes steroids before the race, he can expect to finish ahead of other slightly faster cyclists who would otherwise beat him. Second, let's assume that some chance exists that a doping cyclist will be caught during a given race, but a much higher probability exists that he can use masking techniques that let him get away with PED use. Finally, we'll assume (safely) that most of the top cyclists will make *a lot* more money if they are successful in cycling than they would in any other profession available to them.

Now consider two equally skilled cyclists deciding whether to use PEDs under these conditions. Each knows that his competitor faces the same choice but doesn't want to risk giving away his own strategy by talking to him about it. The cyclists face a Hamlet-like quandary: to dope or not to dope. Just as the prisoners are always best-off ratting on each other, the cyclists' best choice (also known as a "dominant strategy") is always to dope no matter what the other guy does. If one cyclist dopes, the other guy is better off doping because that increases his chances of winning from virtually zero to fifty-fifty. If one cyclist does not dope, the other guy is better off doping because it increases his chances of winning from 50 to nearly 100 percent. The only way doping is not a dominant strategy is if the cyclist in question incurs an extremely high psychological cost from lying and cheating (that is, if lying and cheating make him feel really bad). In that case, the cyclist will choose not to dope because his total payoff (winnings minus psychic costs of lying and cheating) is higher when he does not dope than when he does. Although such cyclists surely exist, it only takes a few less-scrupulous types to create a world in which all the top cyclists are doping.

Why don't the cyclists simply reach a sportsmanlike agreement not to dope? After all, given the negative long-term health consequences of doping, it's in everyone's best interests for both cyclists to abstain. If neither dopes, they each can expect to do about as well relative to each other, and the fans can enjoy an equally competitive (if somewhat slower) race.

The answer is a matter of sheer volume. Although the prisoner's dilemma contains only two agents, who operate in a kind of vacuum, the real-world cyclist's dilemma involves not just two cyclists but hundreds. As long as many of them have access to performance-enhancing technology, only one cyclist needs to begin doping before others (eventually, virtually *all* others) feel that they have to.

Is cycling a true prisoner's dilemma? Has the sport degenerated to the point where you can safely assume that any winner of a major race is doping? Was Armstrong not a villain but merely the king of an era in which competition remained fair but was elevated to enhanced levels?

The length and location of the Tour de France course change every year, but we can compare performance across years by looking at average speed. As equipment improved, the winner's average speed increased steadily and significantly from the race's early years into the mid-1950s. Between 1956, when the Frenchman Robert Walkowiak won at an average speed of about 22.5 miles per hour, and 1985, when the Frenchman Bernard Hinault won at about the same speed, the winning speed rose and fell based mainly on the course.

After 1985, however, racing speed took off to previously unthinkable highs. Since 1991, no cyclist has won the Tour with an average speed of less than 23.8 miles per hour. Certainly, some of the uptick is attributable to technology, but given the rules put in place in the 1990s by cycling's governing body, Union Cycliste Internationale, to limit overly advanced bikes, it seems unlikely that the unprecedented speeds were due to better frames and wheels alone.

The former cyclist Steve Swart recalled the changes in his memoir: "In 1987 and '88, it was one world. In 1994 it had completely changed. The increase in speed was unbelievable. . . . They [weren't] using the same gears as before."[4] Swart had abstained from doping as he raced in the less competitive American tour. When he returned to the European circuit, in 1994, he began injecting EPO. "Look," the once steadfastly antidoping Swart later told a group of young cyclists that included Armstrong's future teammate George Hincapie, "if you're going to make it in this game, you're going to have to do that stuff, simple as that."[5] He seems to have been right: a report by the United States Anti-Doping Agency concluded, "Twenty of the twenty-one podium finishers in the Tour de France from 1999 through 2005 have been directly tied to likely doping through admissions, sanctions, public investigations or exceeding the UCI hematocrit [red blood cell portion] threshold."[6] The Tour winners in 1996, '97, and '98 all used PEDs as well.

In short, then, the incentives to cheat in cycling are—or at least were—so strong that virtually everyone at the top of the sport seems to end up doing it. Although the consensus is that doping in cycling has declined since more aggressive testing and policing were put in place in 2008, there is an equally strong consensus that doping remains a substantial factor in elite cycling. One authority concluded, "The general view is that at the elite level the situation has improved, but that doping is still taking place."[7] The average speed at the Tour de France has stabilized, but it has not dropped from the days of Lance Armstrong and other notorious cheaters. We can safely assume that many winners of top cycling races are doping—or, as an economist would think of it, following the dominant strategy.

Does Crime Pay?

For baseball, meanwhile, the Mitchell Report marked a turning point. Cynics complained that the report was merely a publicity move to distract from the league's lack of interest in taking substantive action against steroids. But the report's release coincided with a sharp decline in steroid use. Before 1996, the five league-leading home run hitters had averaged forty-five home runs or more just three times in over a hundred years. In twelve consecutive seasons beginning in 1996, the top five in each league averaged more than forty-five home runs every year—a total of twenty-four times. At the end of that period, before the 2008 season, the Mitchell Report came out, and home run production dropped off a cliff. In the following six years, the five leading home run hitters didn't average more than forty-five home runs even once.

The Mitchell Report named about eighty players as steroid users. The list identified a number of MVPs and Cy Young Award winners, including Barry Bonds, Roger Clemens, and Jose Canseco. Shortly after the release of the Mitchell Report, reports spread of a second, sealed list of 104 players who had tested positive during an experimental testing period in 2003. Leaks from unnamed sources eventually pointed to the superstars Alex Rodriguez and David Ortiz as being among the ostensibly anonymous 104 positive tests on the second list.

For big stars like these, the incentives to use steroids were not entirely financial. Take Bonds, for instance. Reporters who covered his fall from grace paint a picture of a rabidly jealous man driven to steroid use by his envy of McGwire's and Sosa's spotlight during their home run race in 1998. Bonds began to take performance-enhancing drugs around then, as he knew McGwire and Sosa already were, and became noticeably bulked up. But Bonds was already on track to become a historically great player before his biceps spontaneously doubled in size. In the 1998 season, he significantly outperformed Sosa and matched or edged McGwire using advanced statistical measures of productivity.[8] The contract Bonds signed in 1993 was at the time the richest deal ever for a professional baseball player. By the end of the 1998 season, he had collected three MVP awards, been selected to eight All-Star teams, and won eight Gold Gloves. Bonds had little financial incentive to dope. Rather, his steroid use seems to have been fueled as much by an ego-driven need to secure his place in baseball history. Even perennial All-Star players have a higher level to aspire to, and sometimes it can be enough to set them down the path of using drugs.

The public, though fascinated by Bonds, was less interested in his teammate Bobby Estalella. A career .216 hitter, Estalella shared only two traits with Bonds: they had baseball in their genes (Bonds's father and Estalella's grandfather were both Major League All-Stars), and both were linked to steroids in the Mitchell Report.

Estalella's prisoner's dilemma had different payoffs from Bonds's, but the outcome and the dominant strategy were the same. Estalella was among a sizable tier of players sometimes referred to as AAAA-players: those who have bounced between the major and minor leagues more than a couple of times and spend most of their careers dealing with the fear of demotion. Most are interchangeable in the eyes of fans, but for these players, the financial value of staying in the big leagues is huge. The minimum salary in MLB in 2001 (the year Bonds set the single-season home run record) was $200,000, and the average MLB salary was around $2 million. A player in the minor leagues at that time, by contrast, would have been lucky to earn $75,000 per year. (Today the minimum major-league salary is over $500,000, and the median is over $1 million.) Estalella played in the minor leagues in all but two of the nine years that he saw some major-league action. He earned up to $550,000 per year by staying in the majors much of the time.

Estalella had the option of abstaining from steroids, but doing so would have made it more likely that he would play in minor-league obscurity, ride buses to games, and maybe earn a decent but far from lucrative living. A second option was to take steroids, collect the much higher paychecks that went with playing in the majors, and—at least for a few years—travel to games in chartered jets.[9]

Estalella knew he would most likely never have the chance to earn so much money again. Many other marginal players face the same choice. It doesn't take long for one borderline pro to start using steroids, and then for others to follow. They would prefer not to, and all might agree to stay clean if such an agreement were credible. But when their best financial option for the rest of their lives is on the line, they have a strong incentive to bite the bullet and use steroids to avoid getting left behind. It's a dominant strategy. When a small difference in quality makes a big difference in income, the incentive to cheat becomes very strong.

Trust but Verify, or Just Give Up

When the incentive to take performance-enhancing drugs is strong enough, some athletes will make the wrong choice and corrupt their sport. What can be done about it? Unfortunately, the answer is probably "not much." Two key elements often help clean up prisoner's dilemma–like situations: verifiability and repeated interactions with potential penalties. These approaches, however, are difficult to establish for PED use in sports.

Let's start with verification. "Trust but verify" is a mantra often used by politicians tasked with setting up arms agreements.[10] During the Cold War, for example, the United States and the Soviet Union each built up massive arsenals of nuclear weapons before eventually signing treaties to reduce their respective stockpiles. A prisoner's dilemma ensued in which each nation's best natural strategy was to break the deal and keep building its arsenal—either to use against a weakly defended, treaty-observing enemy or to protect itself against a similarly treaty-defiant one. The treaties therefore needed to stipulate how each side could verify that the other was following the terms. Ultimately the treaties would succeed only if the verification provisions allowing each side to detect cheating were strong enough.

Although the stakes are lower, sports with PED problems have their own verification procedure, drug testing, which they are constantly trying to refine. Testing as verification should theoretically fix the doping problem: just check athletes' urine or blood for illegal substances periodically, and the cheaters will quickly be driven out. But, as any casual fan knows, it's not quite that simple; testing efforts always seem to fall one step behind the latest drug-masking technology.

Every so often, baseball's tests nab an All-Star like Ryan Braun. Meanwhile, though, dozens of other users avoid a positive result. Evidence of this evasion emerges when cheaters who went unnoticed by testing labs are caught by investigators or journalists who piece together the players' connections with distributors. Indeed, MLB reported that of the twenty players—including Braun—who were caught acquiring steroids in the Biogenesis scandal of 2014, only four had previously been identified as users by the league's drug-testing authority.[11]

Still, testing has likely served as a deterrent to some degree; the specter of a failed test must loom especially large for athletes consumed by their public images. But the trickle of sluggers, sprinters, cyclists, and other athletes who are nabbed for steroid use remains unchanged. It's fair to assume that, at least as yet, verification protocols offer an imperfect solution for sports officials looking to combat their athletes' PED prisoner's dilemma. What else can they try?

Stronger punishment sounds like the natural solution: change the payoffs so that cheating is no longer a dominant strategy because the sanctions from getting caught are overwhelming. But in many cases, that approach is unlikely to work. Because testing seems to be so easy for clever dopers to overcome, no penalty, even a severe one, is likely to be sufficient to swing the balance against doping.

Given the limits of any testing-based system, it's tempting to turn to an easier solution: embrace reality. Sports would still be fun to watch if PEDs were allowed. Athletic governing bodies that try to enforce antidrug rules could follow the lead of NCAA men's tennis officials, who simply gave up on regulating cheating. In college tennis, players referee themselves; they call balls in or out, and they determine whether the opponent's serve hit the net on the way over. If a player hits a fantastic serve that the other player cannot return, the returning player can, by the traditional rules of tennis, yell "let." This indicates that the serve hit the net and must be redone. Some lets are obvious, but often these nicks of the net are all but unnoticeable. Many ethically challenged college players fell into the habit of claiming that clean serves that they could not return were actually lets.

This type of cheating became a prisoner's dilemma where even honest kids felt they had to call some dubious lets to keep up with the cheaters they faced. In response, the NCAA eliminated the let—a staple of tennis at all other levels—so that any serve that landed in the service box, regardless of whether it touched the net or not, was considered in play. Surely the NCAA will soon be able to reverse this rule, as improvements in technology are making it affordable to install devices that can identify when a serve hits the net. In other words, once "verify" becomes an option, NCAA tennis can revert to traditional rules without worrying about cheating.

Low-cost net-cord-detection devices would solve the NCAA tennis issue once and for all. The situation is more complicated with PED detection, though, because testers and cheaters are both evolving in a constant cat-and-mouse game. So the only real alternative to the current system is for sports officials to simply throw their hands up and give in to the dilemma. Leaders of leagues particularly plagued by steroids could, like NCAA tennis officials, concede and allow their players to do what they want. As some observers point out, the benefits of PED use are not entirely different from, say, training at altitude (though that argument ignores the long-term health consequences of PED use). More important, those commentators say, is recognizing that all other approaches have failed and that only legalization creates a chance of leveling the playing field for all athletes.[12] Although those who favor this "embrace and accept" strategy still seem to be well in the minority, I suspect that sports fans and athletic governing bodies may slowly put their ethical concerns aside and move toward it. Economically speaking, it's hard to conceive of a more elegant realistic solution.

Is Usain Bolt for Real?

The only other sport that can claim to have been tainted by PED use comparable to that in cycling and baseball must be sprinting.

Well, okay, also weightlifting, and football, and field events like discus. But in any case, steroid use is a major problem in sprinting. Medalists in the sport's highest-profile event, the Olympic men's 100-meter sprint, have repeatedly been linked to steroids over the past three decades, and those who haven't been caught have remained under suspicion simply by association and their inability to prove otherwise. The public's cynicism toward sprinters is reasonable even without the rash of positive tests from big-name sprinters: the 100-meter sprint has seen a readily observable performance uptick, comparable to the performance increases in cycling and baseball. Before the 1988 Olympics, only two Olympians had ever broken ten seconds in the 100-meter dash; since that year, only three medalists have *not* been under ten seconds, and two of those times were run in the wind-hindered 1992 race in Barcelona.

At some point, runners clearly began to face the same prisoner's dilemma as cyclists. That point likely came around 1984, when the infamous Canadian sprinter Ben Johnson first picked up a bronze medal. He went on to win gold in 1988 before being brought down in a widely publicized doping scandal that rocked the sport. The famous American sprinter Carl Lewis, who beat Johnson for gold in 1984, has never been proved to have doped, but he did record a positive drug test result in 1988 for which he was eventually cleared.[13]

Regardless of whether Lewis was or wasn't guilty, plenty of other gold medalists—from Linford Christie in 1992 to Justin Gatlin in 2006—were caught doping at some point in their careers. Even sprinters with completely clean testing records have had fingers pointed at them. Victor Conte, ringleader of the notorious BALCO lab, a primary steroid provider to both sprinters and baseball players, told an Australian newspaper that every runner in the Sydney Olympics 100-meter final was using steroids. Those athletes included two prominent sprinters, Maurice Green and Ato Boldon, who enjoyed successful and ostensibly clean careers. Since the Sydney Games, a leaked letter supposedly written by Boldon to a former coach alleged that Green used steroids; Boldon himself once tested positive, but track and field's governing body cleared him of wrongdoing.

In recent years, the otherworldly Jamaican Usain Bolt dominated sprinting from his emergence in 2005 until his retirement in 2017, rewriting the sport's record books. An athletic freak who has never tested positive, Bolt calmly denied allegations while many of his rivals—such as the Americans Tyson Gay and Justin Gatlin and the Jamaican Asafa Powell—were caught and suspended for steroid use.

Could Bolt truly be clean? Conte doesn't think so: he said in the same interview that he "strongly suspected" Bolt was on steroids. Decisively beating all competition on a level playing field is one thing. But were Bolt's talents *so* great that he could win decisively while running clean against competitors who were cheating? If Bolt was indeed clean, his natural sprinting talent would have had to be like no one else who ever laced up sprinting spikes.

How much of an outlier would Bolt have had to be? To answer this question, I need to establish a couple of baselines. First, I will estimate that using PEDs lowers a given runner's time in the 100-meter dash by at least a tenth of a second and maybe close to a quarter of a second. I say this because winning times in the event dropped by about a quarter of a second between the late 1970s and the late 1980s, which appears to be the period during which steroid use became common.[14]

Second, I will assume that, at any given moment, the fastest man in the world is not typically faster than the second fastest by more than a tenth of a second. The winner of the Olympic finals in the 100-meter dash rarely wins by more than a tenth of a second. Though larger margins of victory were somewhat more common in the pre-steroid era, when few people were organizing their lives around the Olympics, winning by more than a tenth of a second was an anomaly.

Bolt won the finals of the 2008, 2012, and 2016 Olympic 100-meter dashes by twenty, twelve, and eight one-hundredths of a second, respectively. Given that his competitors in the first two races have all since been connected to steroids, to have achieved those winning margins, Bolt would have to have been a quarter to a half second faster than the clean versions of all the other runners.

Moreover, Bolt's best time, 9.58 seconds, is a full fifth of a second better than the best time ever run by any other runner who has not been credibly connected to steroid use.[15] That margin is the largest attained by any world record breaker in the 100-meter dash. Bolt also, with his win in 2008, broke the Olympic record by a wider margin (0.15 seconds) than any previous record breaker had ever achieved. The last time a sprinter broke prior records by so much was when Marion Jones tore up the women's record book in the late 1990s and early 2000s. Jones was later shown to have used PEDs and was stripped of all her major titles. In 1988, Florence Griffith Joyner broke the world records in both the 100- and 200-meter dashes by about a quarter of a second after showing rapid, drastic improvement. She has always been under strong suspicion of using steroids to make that leap, though like Bolt, she has never been proved to have done so and maintains she has always been clean.

Bolt denies PED use in the strongest possible terms. He has said, "I am clean, I'm sure about that. I welcome people to test me every day if necessary to prove it to the world. I have no problem."[16] His coach has said, "We know he is as clean as a whistle."

Unfortunately, these kinds of statements mean almost nothing. Such talk is cheap and is just what athletes who regularly used PEDs said before they were caught. Lance Armstrong, for example, declared publicly and defiantly, "How many times do I have to say it? . . . Well, it can't be any clearer than 'I've never taken drugs,'" and "I have never doped."[17] Serial cheater and liar Alex Rodriguez responded to Katie Couric's question on national television, "For the record, have you ever used steroids, human growth hormone, or any other performance-enhancing substance?" with a simple "No" shortly before he first admitted to taking PEDs. Marion Jones, months before definitive evidence forced her to admit longtime steroid use, stated, "I'm confident in the near future my name will be cleared from this whole situation."

If Bolt truly never took a PED, it is a shame that the cheaters sowed doubts in fans' minds that can never fully be disproved. The world will only know for sure whether Bolt used steroids if he is caught; there is no way to ever be certain he is clean.

Although the odds are astronomically against any sprinter being as much better than the competition as Bolt is, it is theoretically feasible that he is just more of an outlier than anyone who came before. As Ralph Mann, director of sprints and hurdles for USA Track and Field, has argued on Bolt's behalf, "Every once in a while you're going to get a genetic freak among freaks—a Tiger Woods or a Michael Jordan in his sport. And we've got one in Usain Bolt."[18] Anything's possible, I guess.

Why Don't NBA Players Get Caught Using PEDs?

Sprinting, cycling, baseball, football, and weightlifting are all widely known to have massive steroid abuse issues and all fit the prisoner's dilemma framework. With some exceptions when drug testing has been particularly aggressive and successful, top competitors benefited enough from PED use that one can surmise that the winners (and, in many cases, marginal players like Bobby Estalella) are getting chemical assistance. That's because these sports have three important characteristics. First, the value added by PEDs is enough that the best players competing without them cannot outperform second-tier players competing with PEDs. That is, PEDs can be the factor that takes the second- (or third- or fifth- or tenth-) best competitor and allows him or her to win. Second, optimal PED use in these sports raises the visible suspicion that the person has unnatural muscle mass. Ben Johnson, the banned sprinter, was given away by his arms, Barry Bonds by his head and neck, and many Tour de France riders by their freakish legs. Finally, in all these sports, the people who succeed do much better (mostly financially) through their sport than they could possibly hope to do in any other career. The incentives to succeed are overwhelming.

Why do we not hear so much about steroids in hockey, soccer, basketball, golf, tennis, skiing, and bowling? One possibility is that athletes in these sports are more honorable than those in baseball and weightlifting, but that assumption seems pretty naive. And the third characteristic from the list—these athletes make a lot more than they would make in other careers—certainly holds in most of these sports. World-class golfers and basketball players make millions of dollars per year, and even those in skiing and bowling make a lot more than the average person. Given that most of these athletes would not otherwise be investment bankers, it's safe to say that professional sports offer a large step up from what they can make elsewhere.

That leads me to focus on the first two factors: the marginal value of PEDs and the visibility factor. Many people believe that PEDs do not help athletes in endurance sports or in sports that are more "athletic" (such as basketball or tennis) and less muscle based (such as football and cycling). But PEDs can help athletes improve their strength and their recovery from difficult workouts in any sport. A tennis player cannot bulk up like Barry Bonds, because then the player would not be able to chase down drop shots. But smaller doses could help that player's muscles recuperate after a long match or an intense practice session. A well-planned steroid regimen can help almost any athlete. But it is less clear whether the benefits of PEDs to a typical athlete in these situations are enough to outweigh the psychic costs of cheating, the side effects, and the risk of getting caught. The benefits certainly outweigh the costs for *some* athletes, as there are credible reports of PED use in most of the sports mentioned earlier (not bowling). But it appears that a solid majority of athletes do not think the upside of steroids is worth it, because they can do fine without them.[19] Steroid use in these sports is not a prisoner's dilemma, because it is not the dominant strategy for any given player to choose to use PEDs.

Although the cost-benefit calculus is what determines whether PEDs create a prisoner's dilemma in a given sport (yes in cycling and sprinting, no in skiing and hockey), the visibility issue is likely a crucial factor affecting whether PED use becomes a scandal. If the athletes look so freakish that people cannot accept them as natural, fans and analysts take note. Some basketball players and tennis players probably use PEDs, but they use them in smaller doses, to improve recovery and endurance rather than to build huge muscles. Fans and commentators don't see anything unusual. Once in a while, an NBA player gets caught (for example, All-Star Joakim Noah and near-All-Star O. J. Mayo were suspended for PED use), but the NBA's testing regimen is not particularly intense, and PED use is not widely seen as a problem.

Economics offers two conclusions about drug use in sports. First, if you strongly suspect that an athlete is doping, he or she probably is. At least in some muscle-focused sports, the rewards for cheating and lying are huge, and as long as at least a few people are willing to cross that line, others have little choice but to follow. Lance Armstrong, Marion Jones, and others who used PEDs in cycling and sprinting were only following their dominant strategies. Second, just because you don't hear much about drugs in a sport doesn't mean people are not using them to get an edge. Maybe there really isn't much to report, but it's just as likely that nobody is digging deep enough to find out. For athletes, the problem is simple: if a large number of your opponents are cheating and you have no effective way to catch them, you most likely will not win unless you cheat too.

4

Are Athletes Worth All That Money?

Professional athletes make a lot of money. In 2019, the median income for American men twenty-five years or older with full-time jobs was about $52,000.[1] That is, half of the full-time workforce made more than $52,000, and half made less. The players in the four major American sports leagues, as well as players in top international soccer leagues, do a lot better. For instance, the median Major League Baseball salary in 2019 was $1.4 million. Similarly, the median NBA salary in the 2018–2019 season was $2.65 million.[2]

It wasn't always this way. Major League Baseball players in 1964 made a median salary, adjusted for inflation, of $122,000.[3] The median income of all full-time employed male workers in 1964, again adjusted for inflation, was $52,000.[4] An MLB player made about twice as much as a typical American male worker in 1964, but twenty-seven times as much as that same worker in 2019. To put it another way, from 1964 to 2019, the typical American male full-time worker's pay has stayed unchanged, but the typical MLB player's income has grown by a factor of more than eleven.

A visual sense of the stark difference in the pay trajectories of average workers and top professional athletes is shown clearly in graph form (figure 3); the graph focuses on MLB players, but other sports look similar. For both MLB players and what the Census Bureau refers to as "production and nonsupervisory" workers, average pay is set to one in 1967, and all pay figures are adjusted for inflation. Over the

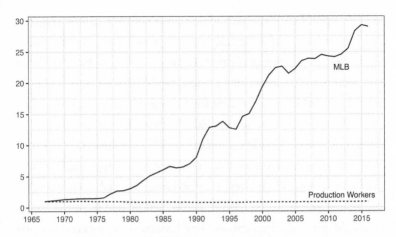

Figure 3. Growth in pay for MLB players and production workers (1967 = 1)
[Illustration by Julio C. Franco]

next fifty years, the nonathletes' pay barely budged from the 1967 level, but MLB pay went up steeply and steadily.

The growth in athletes' pay, and some of the details regarding how that pay has come to grow over time, suggests at least three questions. Why do professional athletes make so much and, in particular, so much more than they used to make? Why do baseball and basketball stars get large guaranteed contracts, while most football stars are one bad season away from losing their million-dollar paychecks? Finally, why do players and owners fight so much over money, occasionally getting into such bitter disagreements that part or all of a season is canceled?

The answers to these questions lie in the stories behind three numbers: $430 million, $53 million, and $580 million, in that order.

The $430 Million Man

As the 2019 baseball season was approaching, Mike Trout was widely considered the best baseball player in the world. Ever since he took the sport by storm in his rookie season of 2012, Trout's statistics had been otherworldly. He had also been relatively injury free, missing a substantial number of games in only one season. He had placed first or second in American League Most Valuable Player voting in every season of his career except for the one where he missed a quarter of the season, when he finished fourth in the voting. On one of my favorite baseball podcasts, *Effectively Wild,* the hosts regularly discussed the degree to which Trout could be handicapped and remain a major-league-quality player. They had long, spirited discussions, for example, about how good Trout would be if he had to run the bases backward, how valuable he would be if he were allowed only one swing each time he came to bat, and (I am not making this up) whether he could fake his death midway through his career, assume a new persona, and be inducted into the baseball Hall of Fame twice. In short, Mike Trout was (and is) an outstanding baseball player.

Shortly before the start of the season, Trout and the Los Angeles Angels agreed to a twelve-year contract for a total of $430 million. This was the largest guaranteed contract in the history of North American sports, and it entitles Trout to an average annual income of almost $36 million until he turns thirty-nine (an age at which few hitters remain productive).

If Trout played in every single Angels game scheduled during the life of the contract, he would have made an average of $211,000 per game. Every time Trout spends a few hours at the ballpark, he takes home four times the median annual salary of a full-time American male worker.

That average American worker might not think Trout is worth his pay. That worker might even say it isn't "fair" that he earns about $25 an hour, has trouble paying his bills, and can't do enough to help his kids get ahead in life, while Trout makes millions for *playing a game.*

Even economists are human, so I can't help but sympathize with that view. A baseball player who excels at his craft does not do nearly as much to serve others as a farmer, a nurse, or a schoolteacher. But those other workers also do not create as much financial value as Trout does.

Trout makes so much money for two reasons: the league has *lots* of money to spend, and he has scarce and valuable skills that make his team better.

In the year Trout signed his record contract, MLB teams brought in a total of almost $11 billion in revenue. ESPN, Fox, and Turner Sports, combined, paid the league nearly $2 billion for the rights to broadcast games nationally.[5] MLB gets another $800 million annually from its streaming and technology arm, MLB Advanced Media.[6]

Ticket sales add billions more. Given that the Angels play in a huge media market, they usually draw large crowds—and though it is hard to determine what fraction of those fans come to see Trout play, star players do draw people in.[7] Some teams hope that signing a player like Trout will pay for itself through a larger local TV deal. This logic doesn't happen to apply in Trout's case, however, because shortly before his rookie season, the Angels signed a huge TV contract that will last through Trout's whole career. But TV revenue is a relevant factor in other large contracts.

Given all that money, what allocates so much of those riches to Trout is just supply and demand. It may not be "fair," but it is what the market will bear. Remember, economics is the study of scarce resources, and the ability to hit forty home runs per season in Major League Baseball is one of the scarcest resources there is.

The semiofficial currency in which baseball talent is valued is "wins." Teams will pay for anything they think will give them more wins. Winning games sells tickets, leads to higher fees for TV rights, and brings in revenue from playoff ticket and merchandise sales.

The market for wins is much like the market for stocks. Investors bet on a stock because they think they will see future returns based on the company's good financial performance. Similarly, MLB teams invest in players if the expected return in terms of wins (which can be translated back into money) is high enough.

Back in 1974, one of the first prominent sports economists, Gerald Scully, was the first (that I know of) to calculate major-league players' value. He estimated that Hank Aaron, the biggest star of that era, would "be the difference between victory and defeat in about 20 games" and was worth $600,000 (in 1971 dollars) to his team. Scully's calculations were extremely innovative at the time, but in the decades that followed, the data on baseball became much better. Sabermetricians—fans and analysts named for the Society for American Baseball Research who set the early standard for advanced statistical analysis of baseball—have become extremely sophisticated at determining players' relative value in terms of how much they increase the expected success of their teams. One statistic they developed that has become a standard for comparing players is "wins above replacement," or WAR. WAR estimates how many fewer games a player's team would win if that player were unavailable and the team instead used a "replacement-level" player. Replacement players are generally the best players in the minor leagues, so they are below average compared with other players in the top league. Modern sabermetricians assign Aaron a WAR of about eight for his play during the 1971 season, meaning that the Atlanta Braves would have won eight fewer games that year had Aaron been replaced by a right fielder from the top of the minor-league hierarchy.[8]

Throughout his career, Mike Trout has been at least as good as Aaron was in 1971, averaging eight to ten wins above replacement for his team every season. In 2018, as Trout's previous contract neared its end, the Angels wanted to ensure they could continue benefiting from his abilities. Although they had Trout locked in for two more seasons, he could have become a free agent at the end of 2020, meaning he could go to any team he wanted. Looking at other recent contracts and projecting future league revenues, the Angels could have figured that if Trout became a free agent, he would be offered contracts paying $50 million or more per season. This is because the baseball market, using methods similar to the stock market, had determined that the price of one expected win was about $10.5 million, according to an estimate in 2017 (which also projected the price would rise to $12 million by 2019).[9] Given Trout's eight-plus win production, the $36 million per year he receives can be viewed as a steep discount (a point I will return to).

So Trout is well worth his $430 million, or $36 million per year. But why weren't Ted Williams and Mickey Mantle, superstars of yesteryear, worth $36 million per year when they played? Each was the highest-paid major leaguer at some point, earning $90,000 per year.[10] Adjusted for inflation, that is the equivalent of about $760,000 (Mantle's 1962 salary) or $885,000 (Williams's 1951 salary) in 2019 (the first year of Trout's contract). Although Mantle and Williams certainly made good money, they were paid not even one-fortieth of what Trout earns. MLB players who earned the equivalent of Mantle's or Williams's peak pay in 2019 include Chris Hermann, a journeyman catcher with a career batting average of about .200; Alex Wilson, a relief pitcher who generally comes into the game when the outcome is largely decided; and J. B. Shuck, an outfielder who has not played in more than half his team's games in any year since a promising 2013 rookie season. In that same season, an arbitrator awarded Tommy Pham, a solid five-year veteran center fielder with career highs of 73 RBI and 23 home runs, a salary of $4.1 million. So a solid modern player makes about five times as much as Williams and Mantle made at their peaks.[11]

This pay inflation is not unique to baseball. Similar increases have taken place in all American team sports, in European football leagues, and in individual sports such as tennis, golf, and auto racing. What changed? Why has the level of pay in baseball and other sports increased by double-digit multiples over the last fifty years? The increase can be explained by three economic factors: technological change, competition, and income distribution.

From the days of Williams and Mantle to the present, technology has exerted what the economist Sherwin Rosen dubbed a "superstar effect." National and local networks pay billions of dollars to broadcast major-league games, and MLB makes almost a billion dollars from internet rights. Obviously it was not always this way. In the 1950s and '60s, the internet did not exist yet. Most households had television sets, but broadcasting live sporting events was difficult and expensive, and the quality was limited. Instead of watching on forty-plus-inch high-definition screens, people saw sports on small black-and-white sets. Reception in much of the country was blurry at best.

Over time, as broadcasts got better through the introduction of color, more camera angles, instant replay, and other improvements, viewers' best option migrated from local, in-person events to watching games on TV. Most sports fans would agree that the best baseball to watch is the major leagues. But in the times of Mantle and Williams, a fan's choice was between a poor view of the best games and a better view of an inferior game—like American Legion, semipro, or minor-league baseball—at the local ballpark. Mantle and Williams were superstars, but watching them play was not always the best option. With today's high-definition TV, though, Mike Trout and contemporary superstars get a much bigger share of the baseball audience and so can command much larger salaries. As Rosen and another economist, Allen Sanderson, put it, "A star player is worth only a few dollars more per spectator than an ordinary player. There are lots of spectators."[12]

Not only is this superstar effect not limited to baseball—local leagues for other sports have also been overtaken by people watching the world's best on TV—but it is not limited to sports. Consider Kevin Hart. He began as a successful stand-up comedian playing small venues. If he had been born a few decades earlier, that is probably how he would have spent most of his career. But thanks to mass media like film and cable television, Hart makes millions doing movies and stand-up specials on TV. *Forbes* estimates he earned $57 million in one recent year, an unheard-of amount for a comedian from a previous era who could make money only by touring.[13] Even superstars of classical music can cash in on the superstar effect. The cellist Yo-Yo Ma makes millions of dollars each year from his recordings and his advertising deals with Apple and Hyundai. In an earlier era, when classical musicians had to build their audiences one show at a time, there was not nearly such an extreme difference between the most famous cellist and one comparably talented; both played concerts before local audiences. In short, technological changes have expanded the reach of great musicians, comedians, and athletes alike, raining down riches on the superstars.

The second reason Mike Trout makes so much more than Ted Williams could ever dream of making is a seminal driver of economic activity: competition. Williams, Mantle, and baseball players of their era can partly blame their meager earnings on Oliver Wendell Holmes, who was chief justice in 1922 when the U.S. Supreme Court ruled in *Federal Baseball Club v. National League.* Holmes's opinion in that case held that the Sherman Antitrust Act of 1890, which barred monopolistic and anticompetitive practices by American corporations, did not apply to MLB because its "business is giving exhibitions of baseball, which are purely state affairs."[14]

This ruling was still in effect in the spring of 1956, when Mantle was on his way to earning his first Most Valuable Player Award, and Williams—though in the late stages of his storied career—was having another All-Star season. While Mantle and Williams were busy on the field, the University of Chicago economist Simon Rottenberg was busy doing research. That June, Rottenberg published "The Baseball Players' Labor Market" in the *Journal of Political Economy*, and the academic field of sports economics was born.[15] Rottenberg identified the key constraint on players' salaries as the baseball teams' exclusive rights to players, an agreement among teams known as the Reserve Clause, which severely limited the players' options. Under the Reserve Clause, even after a player's contract had run out, his team retained exclusive rights to his services. Such a player, Rottenberg wrote, "may withdraw from organized baseball and follow some other calling, but he may not choose freely among bidders . . . within baseball." Rottenberg went on to argue that the justifications for limiting player freedom (for example, that "high-revenue teams will contract all the stars, leaving the others only the dregs of the supply") were unsupported, and even small-market teams could remain competitive. His prediction turned out to be largely accurate.

Rottenberg's paper generated an explosion of papers about sports economics. It also, thanks to Curt Flood and Marvin Miller, presaged an explosion in baseball salaries. Flood was a very good, if not great, baseball player of the 1960s who thought that being tied to the team that drafted him was unfair. When the Saint Louis Cardinals traded Flood to the Philadelphia Phillies, he sued baseball for the right to be a free agent. The case again went to the Supreme Court, which again ruled that the Sherman Act did not apply to baseball. But the Flood decision was more tenuous than the earlier decision, and Miller, the president of the MLB Players' Association, was able to exploit this development. Thanks to Miller's work on behalf of a few other players in succeeding years, teams' rights to permanent control of a player were eradicated.

Starting in 1975—when Miller's efforts led to the end of baseball's Reserve Clause in an arbitration case—American professional sports leagues and their players' unions collectively bargained the rights of players to move from one team to another. In all sports, after at least a few years of league experience, players now become free agents when their contracts expire, and they can then sign with any team they like.

Trout had a third choice beyond the two that were available to Mantle and Williams—play for the team to which they were assigned, or quit baseball entirely—he could become a free agent and sign with whatever team offered him the best deal. Needless to say, that third option made a big difference in his negotiation with the Angels.

The effects of competition on baseball salaries are clear from the rapid rise in player pay after free agency was introduced. Jim "Catfish" Hunter, the first free agent, signed with the New York Yankees in 1974 for $4.5 million over five years. This contract was far more lucrative than any that had been signed before. Between 1964 and 1974, the top salary in the league rose by 138 percent, but in the next ten years, with the advent of free agency, it rose by 700 percent.[16] That increase, the fastest the league has ever seen, was mirrored by increases after free agency began in other leagues, such as the NFL and the NBA.

The third reason Trout makes so much more than Mantle or Williams (in addition to technology and competition) is income inequality. At the same time that technology and the superstar effect were increasing pay for top athletes and other stars relative to their less accomplished peers, those trends were having the same effect on the U.S. economy (and many other countries' economies as well).

Over the past several decades, the American rich have gotten richer. The fraction of American income earned by the top 1 percent of all wage earners rose from around 10 percent in the 1960s and '70s to nearly 25 percent in recent years.[17] From 1970 to 2011, the average pay for CEOs of firms in the S&P 500 grew (after adjusting for inflation) from just over $1 million to just under $11 million.[18] The pay of top lawyers, hedge fund managers, and other executives went up by similar amounts.[19]

These rich people increase the demand for expensive tickets and experiences at sports events—both through their enormous wealth and through their control of the tax-deductible expense accounts of the businesses they run. Consider the New York Yankees, the team with perhaps the greatest number of rich fans. Field box seats at Yankee Stadium are great seats. In 1970, they cost an inflation-adjusted $26 in 2019 dollars.[20] The same tickets cost $300 in 2019—more than eleven times as much.

The Yankees and other teams have figured out even more lucrative ways to pamper the 1 percent. Luxury boxes at Yankee Stadium, which provide tickets, food, extremely comfortable seating, HDTV (you came all the way to the park, but you can still see the game better on TV), and Wi-Fi for twenty-two people, run between $8,500 and $20,000 per game. If the Yankees sell a few of those boxes each home game, they can afford to pay another superstar an eight-figure salary.[21]

That willingness to pay for great Yankees tickets has skyrocketed as the wages of fans who want those tickets have skyrocketed—which, in turn, has been a big contributor to the Yankees' skyrocketing payroll. It's a virtuous circle of the rich getting richer.

In short, Mike Trout came along at the right time relative to Mickey Mantle and Ted Williams. By the time Trout arrived in the major leagues, technology had greatly widened baseball's audience, players had been freed from the indentured servitude of the Reserve Clause, and the United States had plenty of extremely rich people looking to show themselves off at sporting events. Trout has 430 million reasons to be grateful for these trends.

The $360 Million Contract Hole

In 2020, about a year and a half after Mike Trout signed the largest contract in baseball history, quarterback Patrick Mahomes signed a $502 million contact with the Kansas City Chiefs of the National Football League—the largest contract in NFL history.[22] Like Trout compared with Mantle, Mahomes got a huge premium relative to Johnny Unitas and other NFL quarterbacks of yesteryear. One analysis showed that the average NFL salary grew by a factor of twelve, adjusted for inflation, from 1969 to 2013.[23] The divide has only widened since then.

Even though Trout's contract seems a bit smaller than Mahomes's, most people would (at least financially) prefer to be in Trout's position. If at some point during the life of the contract, Trout had an injury that made him unable to play baseball, he would still get his $36 million per year. If he decided he didn't really enjoy playing baseball anymore and was just going to go through the motions to fulfill his contract, he would still get the $36 million every year. His $430 million is guaranteed.

Mahomes, meanwhile, gets his $502 million only if things fall his way. The Chiefs can cut him at any time and save about $30 million per year from that point forward. Mahomes is guaranteed only $141 million in total, or about $360 million less than the contract's maximum value.

Why does this $360 million gulf exist? Why can the Chiefs drop Mahomes and save millions, while the Angels will have to pay Trout no matter what? The difference in the size and guarantees of NFL contracts compared with contracts in other sports presents a difficult puzzle.

The natural response to the difference is to say that since injury rates are higher in the NFL, it makes sense that football teams would be reluctant to guarantee large contracts. But that response is, in a word, wrong.

Two features of long-term contracts explain the difference in guaranteed money between Trout and Mahomes. First, such contracts allow teams and players to plan. The Chiefs' knowledge that Patrick Mahomes will be their quarterback for several years, and the Angels' knowledge that Mike Trout will be their center fielder for several years, allow both teams to market tickets and merchandise using the players' respective images, sell expensive apparel with their respective names and numbers on it, and make decisions about other players that complement a great quarterback or center fielder.

Second, teams effectively act as their players' insurance companies. Athletes' skills are like your house or your health: they represent a huge part of an athlete's total assets. If something happens to Mahomes's ability to play football or Trout's ability to play baseball and they don't have long-term contracts, they're in big trouble. Just as most people choose to buy health and home insurance, Mahomes and Trout likely want insurance policies on their athletic abilities. Those payments might come in very handy someday—as they did for a prior holder of the NFL's largest contract, Colts quarterback Andrew Luck, who earned millions of dollars despite missing the entire 2017 season.

Restated in economic terms, people who buy health or home insurance are *risk averse*. They prefer to pay some amount of money to insure themselves against a terrible outcome. For example, maybe your house is worth $500,000, and there is a 0.1 percent chance it will be destroyed this year. You are probably willing to pay $1,000 to insure your house this year, even though your expected loss is only $500 (0.1 percent times the loss of $500,000).

When it comes to player contracts, team owners are equivalent to the insurance company, and athletes are the homeowners.[24] The team holds a diversified portfolio of football talent assets in the form of a set of players. Any one player might have an injury or an off year or lose his ability to play well. If that player has a long-term contract, the team takes the hit. It hurts the team, but it hurts the team less than it would hurt the player. Meanwhile, another player might overperform, and the team gets to keep him at the contracted salary for the next season instead of paying him the raise he could earn on the open market. Each player gives up some potential profit so that the team will take on the risk.

That arrangement works for the players, and it works for the teams too—but only if the long-term contracts pay less than what teams would pay if the players were free agents each year. That is, players have to give the team a discount to get the insurance policy, just as you pay an insurance premium that is, on average, profitable for the insurance company.

Okay, I get it—this is the point that's hard to swallow, because it is hard to make the case that $430 million is a discount, even for a player like Mike Trout. But it is. Writers who analyze baseball contracts have shown that players sign for less than their current value to guarantee a long-term income stream. Typically, a star will take a 10 percent discount off his true value in exchange for more guaranteed years.[25]

With these ideas in mind, let's get back to the puzzle of why Trout gets more insurance than Mahomes. Our model of insurance would actually predict the opposite; because the likelihood of a serious injury in football is much greater than in baseball, football teams should be willing to insure their players *more* than baseball teams. Remember: though a team will be extremely unhappy if it owes millions to a player who cannot play, the team is not nearly as unhappy as the player would be if he had to suffer the financial consequences. That football is more dangerous, and football teams have bigger rosters than baseball teams (thus spreading a team's risk over a larger set of players), suggests that football teams should provide more insurance than baseball teams. Mahomes, knowing he has a greater risk of injury, will give his team more of a discount if the team insures his earnings than Trout would be willing to give.

Put another way, an insurance company takes all the downside risk out of your homeownership. Guaranteed contracts take all the downside risk out of athletes' earnings. The value of that insurance should be greater for a football player, and as a result, an economist would expect (all else being equal) more guarantees to football players.

So if baseball players need insurance less than football players, why do they get more of it? Why did the Angels take all of Mike Trout's risk, but the Chiefs take only a small portion of Pat Mahomes's downside risk?

Though it's impossible to prove why baseball players are better insured, I have a hypothesis that squares with the facts and with basic economics. Playing football is painful and difficult, and players must be given stronger extrinsic rewards to willingly endure the ordeal. Perhaps this idea was expressed best by the former NFL lineman Ross Tucker: "In 2004 I played the last four games of the season for the Buffalo Bills knowing I had a herniated disc in my back. I did it because of a sense of duty to my teammates, because we were winning and, most importantly, because I had a substantial playing time bonus if I were to play over 80 percent of the offensive snaps, which I fortunately was able to hit."[26]

Teams will be reluctant to guarantee big contracts if doing so leads players to be less willing to give their all. A player might ask himself why he works so hard when he gets paid the same either way.

So one theory that would reconcile the difference in the amount of insurance provided in baseball and football could be that it is simply harder to play football than to play baseball, and therefore financial incentives to perform are more important. Mike Trout and his teammates do not need the same financial incentive as Patrick Mahomes to play their hardest.

Contracts may insure players against financial loss, but they cannot insure against the deteriorated quality of life that befalls many retired NFL veterans who took too many hits. Maybe a wide receiver would simply not be willing to jump for a ball in the middle of the field and expose himself to a monster hit from the secondary if he didn't need a few more great plays to make sure he stayed on the roster the next year.

The NFL has seen several recent retirements by relatively young and productive football players. The most prominent retiree was Andrew Luck, a superstar quarterback for the Indianapolis Colts and a hometown favorite of ours at Stanford, who quit before turning thirty, walking away from the opportunity to earn tens of millions of dollars. These decisions suggest that teams need constant incentives to keep players from taking the safer way out on the field. Mike Trout does not have to put himself in those dangerous situations, which likely explains why the Angels are less worried about paying him a ton of money for more than a decade. To be sure, economists have uncovered some evidence of "shirking" by baseball, basketball, and soccer players after signing large, long-term contracts—but the evidence is inconsistent, and the amount of shirking detected is generally not large.[27]

In sports as in life, the amount and the way people are paid come down to balancing risk and insurance. The more difficult a job is, the more a person has to be given incentives to do it. Just as employees with crummy jobs have to be watched and run the risk of losing their jobs if they don't perform, football players have to be given extrinsic motivation to put themselves in harm's way. Those economic realities work well for Mike Trout, but they could cost Patrick Mahomes as much as $360 million.

How to Flush $580 Million Down the Toilet

Professional teams and players can agree that players are worth large amounts of money and that it makes sense, to varying degrees, to insure players' careers. The NBA has the highest average salary of the major American sports leagues. NBA owners may not love paying out the millions they do, but the owners are getting a good return on their money. Why, then, did the NBA owners and players have a fight that led them to, essentially, throw $580 million into a garbage can in the fall of 2011? The answer is three simple letters: CBA.

Major American sports leagues exist thanks to arrangements made between team owners (and the managers they employ) and the athletes who play the games. The teams no longer have monopoly rights over a player's whole career. Players in every sport can become free agents after some point, and they have other rights to avoid exploitation before they are eligible for free agency. The players could simply work out contracts individually with teams, and there would be a labor market not that different from the market for lawyers, bankers, or architects.

Unlike most of these other groups, however, and largely as a result of the history of exploitation in sports, athletes throughout American professional team sports have voted to form unions. This creates two levels of negotiation in each sport: individual teams and players negotiating contracts, and the owners as a group negotiating an overall deal with the players' union.

Why would either group want that second level? Under American law, it doesn't matter if the teams want to do it this way or not. The National Labor Relations Act of 1935 gives workers the right to form a union. Once they do, the union bargains on behalf of the players with the teams to iron out the all-important CBA, or collective bargaining agreement.

The union and the CBA provide a useful service to all involved. The players have an advocate that acts on their behalf to avoid exploitation, and the owners, through the commissioner's office, can negotiate as a group to make sure their interests are also looked after.

But *collective* bargaining takes the market out of the equation—and from an economics perspective, that can cause problems. CBAs generally set minimum salaries, pension arrangements, maximum contract lengths (at least in the NBA), restrictions on free agency early in a career, team salary caps (in the NBA, NFL, and NHL), and many other details.

And then there's the money. The NBA players' union and the NBA owners have to agree on how to split the billions of dollars they bring in. The NBA CBA expired after the 2010–2011 season, a year in which the NBA claimed total revenues of $4 billion. That is more than $100 million per team and nearly $10 million per player. Compare the implications of splitting that money 50/50 between owners and players versus giving 55 percent to the players and 45 percent for the owners. The second scenario provides the average owner with $6.7 million less per year and gives the average player $556,000 more. Both sides clearly have a lot of incentive to negotiate hard over the CBA.

In deciding how to negotiate, players and owners need to understand their best alternative to a negotiated agreement, or BATNA. In other words, they need to know their next best option. Remember how if the Angels didn't offer Mike Trout enough money, he could count on another MLB team making a generous offer? This meant that his BATNA with the Angels was pretty close to the $430 million over twelve years that he received from them. If it were very different, he would not have accepted that offer, or the Angels would not have made it.

The NBA players' union BATNA when negotiating a CBA with the owners is not very good. The owners have leases on big arenas, huge TV contracts, a brand name that brings in customers, and many other assets that turn players' talents into cash. The players cannot replicate this outside a deal with the NBA owners (though basketball players try to do so during a CBA dispute in the movie *High Flying Bird*). Any other arrangement, such as the players doing things other than basketball or going off to play in other countries or local leagues, would cut their income to a small fraction of NBA pay.

The owners' BATNA when negotiating a CBA with the players' union is equally unattractive. The players are, by a huge margin, the best and most marketable collection of basketball talent in the world. If the NBA tried to put nonunion players on the court (in union parlance, if they hired "scabs"), their TV contracts would be nullified, ticket revenue would fall off a cliff, and merchandise sales would collapse. Many would be stuck supporting big arenas that had suddenly become white elephants.

A favorite metaphor for the value created by two sides that bring unique assets to an agreement is the "size of the pie." When the two sides have a lot to gain by working together, the pie is bigger. But if the people entitled to slices of the pie argue over how big their slices should be, they often run the risk of shrinking the whole thing. CBA negotiations fit this metaphor perfectly (though readers may feel free to use another, equally apt metaphor: killing the goose that lays the golden egg).

As the NBA players' union and the NBA owners negotiated the CBA, they had to work out a lot of details. But let's focus on a single point: how much would owners spend on player salaries? The owners wanted to reduce those salaries by $400 million per year.

That may seem like a big reduction, but there is no single right way to divide the pie. If either side were to walk away, the pie would shrink from $4 billion to a small fraction of that. Each side can thus credibly say to the other, "You better give us what we're asking for, because you are nothing without us," to which the other side can credibly reply, "The same goes for you, so you give us what *we* want." The inability to agree led to the owners "locking out" the players— that is, canceling the season until a new CBA was worked out.

By the time the sides agreed to a new CBA, in December 2011, the season was shortened. The lost revenue—that is, the shrinkage of the pie for the season—was in the hundreds of millions of dollars: $580 million, by my estimate.[28] That was money the teams and players would never get back. The economic damage overall was even greater, as fans lost out on the value of enjoying games, and people who work at games lost the chance to make money.

This fighting over the pie within a relationship is certainly not limited to basketball. Negotiating CBAs is difficult in all major American sports, and all have seen work stoppages as the players and owners fought over how to share the pie. The same dynamic goes on in other union negotiations as well. Steelworkers, autoworkers, teachers, and others go on strike or get locked out (or threats of strikes and lockouts are made) as new contracts get negotiated. Occasionally this leads to the shutting down of factories and employees scrambling to put food on their table. Usually, after a bit of brinksmanship, a deal gets done before a shutdown occurs. But sometimes both sides lose a lot of money until they come to an agreement and get the business back on track.

Five hundred and eighty million dollars is a lot of money to waste, $360 million is a lot for one person in an injury-prone game to put at risk, and $430 million is a lot of money to pay a man to play a game. But all these amounts reflect the value athletes create in the modern, internet- and TV-enabled world. In a world where the rich are getting vastly richer, the very best athletes are extremely lucky to have been born when they were.

5

Why Do Athletes Use Their
Least Successful Moves So Often?

The garage door was open one summer afternoon at my home on the sprawling Stanford University campus. A light breeze kept the garage cool as the competitive fires heated up toward the end of the fourth game in a best-of-five Ping-Pong battle between my son, David, and me. Though I was once the household king of the Ping-Pong table, David had surpassed me and was a point away from handing me another demoralizing defeat. After a brief rally, I hit a weak shot to David's forehand that I immediately knew he would try to smash for a winner. David's forehand smash is more reliable when he aims crosscourt, and I leaned that way, guessing he would hit to his stronger side. Instead the ball sped down the line behind me. Game and match to David.

Ping-Pong is just a game in our house. David and I can be overly intense about it, but ultimately we play just for fun. Nonetheless, the point at the end of that match illustrates how a game can become game theory. The choices that David made about whether to drive the forehand crosscourt or down the line, and I made about whether to lean left or right, were based on our subconscious application of principles from the economic field of game theory. In economics terms, we each wanted to maximize our utility—in this case, maximize our chances of winning the point—while recognizing that the other player was making calculated, strategic, and selfish choices in his attempt to do the same.

An economist would say that deciding where to hit and how to lean constituted a "mixed-strategy equilibrium." With time and practice, David and I have learned what probability to assign to each choice the other will make while trying to vary our own choices in a roughly random matter. David does not always go crosscourt, even though that's his better shot, because if he did, I would always be waiting there. Sometimes he goes down the line, but since he's not as good that way, he does it just enough to keep me guessing. In the equilibrium we have worked out, David is equally successful, on average, whichever way he hits, and I am equally successful, on average, whichever way I lean.

It's not hard to find mixed strategies in places that sports fans actually care about. Game theory may sound esoteric (and sometimes—okay, most of the time—it is), but once you have some understanding of it, you will never again look at a soccer game, tennis match, or baseball game in the same way. In each of these sports, and most others, success hinges on optimally implementing a "mixed strategy" that relies crucially on two things: knowing how often to choose each strategy, and randomly mixing the strategies so that you remain unpredictable.

Kicking and Diving with a Purpose

One high-profile example of a mixed-strategy equilibrium occurs in the penalty kicks and shootouts that often decide important soccer matches. Though penalty shootouts have little in common with the on-field game action, they are a traditional way of settling elimination games that remain tied when the clock officially runs out. Italy has twice made it to a World Cup final only to see the result decided by penalties, losing in 1994 to Brazil and winning in 2006 against France. The UEFA Champions League, club soccer's biggest competition, had eleven finals decided by shootouts between 1980 and 2020. In international tournaments and other soccer leagues and tournaments, penalty shootouts are the standard way to break a tie at the end of regulation time. Given that shootouts decide games with such high stakes, a fan unfamiliar with soccer might assume them to be intricately strategized matches that pit opponents' key players against one another in a tense battle of pure skill. But that's a wildly romanticized description. Shootouts at the highest level of play involve little more than luck and an ability to control one's nerves.

In a standard shootout, teams alternate taking penalty kicks. Each team gets five kicks, though the game can end sooner if one team gains a decisive advantage, and additional kicks are made as long as the game remains tied. Kicks are taken twelve yards from the goal, with the goalie the only defender. Shot takers have essentially three options: shoot left, shoot right, or shoot straight. Similarly, goalies can either dive left, dive right, or remain in the center. Because the shooter takes his shot from so close to the goal, the goalie does not have time to read and react to the shot and must guess which way to dive while the kicker is still approaching the ball. Game theorists classify penalty kicks as "simultaneous move" games, because both players make their decisions without knowing what choice their opponent will make.

Just like my family Ping-Pong battle, the players in a shootout are forced to use the information they have about themselves and their opponents to make a very simple tactical decision. Shoot left, shoot right, or shoot straight? Dive right, dive left, or don't dive at all?

Let's begin with a simplified scenario. Assume the kicker has only two choices, kick left or kick right, and the goalie also has two: dive left or dive right.[1] Suppose the goalie is equally good at diving each way, and if he dives in the direction of the kick, he has a 50 percent chance of making the save. Suppose, too, that all shooters are right-footed and are a bit more accurate shooting to their left than to their right.[2] Let's assume, then, that a player will put his shot on target 96 percent of the time if he kicks left and 80 percent of the time if he kicks right. Your first thought might be that the kicker should always kick left, because that is where he has the best chance of making the shot.

Of course, that theory doesn't work, because then the goalie will always dive left, and the kicker's success rate will be 48 percent: he will get the shot in the right place 96 percent of the time, and the goalie will save it half the time. Now the 80 percent chance on a shot to the right looks like a much better option.

In reality, however, neither side should ever be a more attractive option than the other. In equilibrium, the kicker must have an equally likely chance of scoring whichever way he kicks, and the goalie must have an equally likely chance of making the save whichever way he dives. The underlying logic is quite intuitive: if the odds of success were higher in one direction, the kicker would increase the probability of going in the direction where he is more successful, and the goalie would do the same.

Starting from the 96 percent and 80 percent accuracy figures for shots to the left and right, respectively, and the 50 percent save rate for a correct guess by the goalie, the optimal strategies for this theoretical kicker and goalie can be derived with a little math. The calculations are fairly simple, but the concepts, which were first articulated by the mathematician John von Neumann (who also made seminal contributions to the creation of nuclear weapons) and the economist Oskar Morgenstern, and refined by John Nash (who was famously portrayed by Russell Crowe in *A Beautiful Mind*), required deep mathematical insight. I'll spare you the manipulation of the numbers, but trust me: the math predicts that a goalie playing under the parameters I have described will dive to the kicker's left about 64 percent of the time and to the kicker's right about 36 percent of the time. Because the kicker is more accurate to the left, the goalie knows that diving that way is more useful—the goalie's dive stops 48 percent of shots to the left and only 40 percent to the right. But, of course, he must dive to the kicker's right enough to prevent him from aiming in that direction every time. The kicker, on the other hand, should find it optimal to kick left 45 percent of the time and kick right 55 percent of the time. Though he is better at shooting left, the kicker has to consider the goalie's tendency to neutralize that strength by diving more often in that direction. Because of that decision by the goalie, the kicker is actually better off going right—his weaker side—a bit more than half the time.

So how often does the kicker score? In this example, the probability of converting the goal is 65 percent no matter which way the kicker aims. If the goalie dives to the kicker's left, he is out of luck for the accurate 80 percent of kicks aimed right, but he reduces the kick's success rate to 48 percent when it goes left. If you add up those probabilities and weight them by the rates at which the hypothetical kicker goes left and right, you get the kicker's 65 percent success rate. If you calculated the probability of success for the goalie diving to the kicker's right, you would get the same number.

This is the best both players can do, *provided the other is strategic about it*. What would happen if the kicker were, for example, to say to himself, "I'm good at kicking to my left—I should do that more often," and began kicking 60 percent of his shots left while the goalie continued to dive to the kicker's left 64 percent of the time? For a while, the change would make no difference. Remember that the goalie has set his probability such that he is equally likely to stop a shot no matter which way he dives. In fact, if the kicker started kicking *all* his shots left, his probability of success would remain 65 percent as long as the goalie did not adjust his strategy. But if the goalie caught on that the kicker went left 60 percent of the time, he would be able to decrease the kicker's overall shot success percentage to about 60 percent by diving to the kicker's left all the time.

You might think the goalie and kicker can't work all the math out and both end up just kicking and diving to the kicker's left a lot. To some extent, you would be right, because, of course, the players do not use Excel Solver, as I did, to figure out how often to go one way or the other.

But through trial and error, as well as advice from more experienced teammates and coaches, top soccer players do a remarkably good job of getting the directional breakdown almost exactly right. The economist Ignacio Palacios-Huerta has become an expert on the economics of soccer, and his work includes a paper analyzing 1,417 penalty kicks in professional soccer games around the world.[3] He found that soccer players choose their directions almost as well as they would if they had Excel to help them. As game theory would predict, kickers are successful at the same rate whether they kick left or right, and goalies are also equally successful no matter which way they dive.

To economists, this finding is not too surprising, because we believe that people who have strong incentives to do something will find the best possible way to do it. The financial and personal returns to scoring (or stopping) goals and winning soccer games are very high in many settings. An athlete who did not maximize his chances of getting the best outcome on each penalty kick would put himself at a big disadvantage in a world where the very best get tremendous pay and adulation, while those who just miss stardom are essentially nobody.

When you next watch a penalty kick on TV or at a stadium, remember that the players are implicitly doing a lot of math to maximize their chances of winning. And if you get out on the soccer field, remember to mix it up when you take a shot on goal.

The Mind Games of the Tennis Serve

From an economist's perspective, using soccer to demonstrate mixed strategies is almost unfair. Penalty kicks are exactly the type of environment we would design in a laboratory to test our models of mixed strategies, so if the theories don't work there, they probably never will. Other games, though, have a similar one-on-one nature but are more complicated. Do our models work there, too?

They do if two economists play. Let's turn to tennis, my favorite competitive sport. Though my glory days as a four-year letterman on the Nutley Maroon Raiders tennis team and as two-time champion of the Forest Lake Camp tennis tournament are increasingly distant memories, I still get out on the court with other middle-aged men a couple of times a week. One of my regular singles opponents is a world-renowned economist who does research in game theory. In those matches especially, I have to get my strategy right, or else I am at a big disadvantage.

Like many players, I use a serve-and-volley strategy on many points. That is, I hit my first serve and then rush in behind the ball. If I rush the net quickly enough, my opponent will have to decide what kind of shot to hit before seeing whether I am coming in or not. But the strategy must be deployed in much the way that penalty kickers choose which direction to aim, because if the server uses it too often, his opponent will consistently execute one of the types of returns designed to beat a serve and volley: either a lob over the server's head or a hard shot down one of the sidelines.

One difference exists between this situation and the penalty kicks. Goalies and penalty kickers have a long time between each penalty kick, and they almost always face a new opponent the next time it happens. Even in a shootout to break a tie, the kicker changes with each kick. So, in practice, it's really not a big deal if a pattern develops. As long as the directional choices follow the optimal percentage, things will work out in the long term. Even if a kicker decides to kick to his left twice, to his right once, then left twice, right once, and so on, it will take a long time for anyone to notice this pattern because he faces a different goalie each time.

But in my tennis matches, I serve at least four (and usually more) points in a row during ten or more service games against the same opponent. In these matches, I serve and volley on about one-third of the points. If I adopted a no-no-yes pattern for rushing the net, I would obtain my ideal ratio of serve and volleys, but my opponent would eventually see the pattern and start lobbing on every third point. The effectiveness of my serve and volley would be greatly reduced. So I have figured out a little trick that I generally reserve for matches with my game theorist opponent: I run the stopwatch on my wristwatch for a few minutes before each service game and stop it randomly. The last three digits of the readout give me three random numbers, and I rush the net on those points in the game. For example, if I stop my watch at 2:13.47, I rush the net on the third, fourth, and seventh points.[4]

Am I just a compulsive economist, or do professional tennis players, whose games people actually care about, worry about these issues too? As you probably guessed, they do. A tennis match is one long sequence of mixed-strategy games. Before each shot, the player has to decide whether to go left or right, whether to hit a drop shot or not, whether to charge the net behind his shot, and so forth.

Given enough data, economists could study all these choices and see whether tennis players are maximizing their chances of winning points. But it's impossible to control for all the relevant factors on some choices tennis players make. The economists Mark Walker and John Wooders limited their exploration of mixed strategies in tennis to the server's placement of his serve on the left or right side of the service box and this decision's effect on the server's eventually winning the point.[5] Walker and Wooders studied only a handful of matches from major championships in which the stakes were high and the players were familiar with each other.[6] Across these matches, they found that the players were equally likely to win a point serving to the right as they were serving to the left. They concluded that tennis players randomize their serve direction to maximize their chances of winning the point, ultimately settling into a mixed-strategy equilibrium.

But did players do this in the optimal way? Did they ensure that they did not settle into a pattern their opponent might discern? This was the question picked up by Shih-Hsun Hsu, Chen-Ying Huang, and Cheng-Tao Tang, economists at National Taiwan University. After replicating Walker and Wooders's findings across a greater number of matches, this time including data from major women's and junior players' tournaments as well, Hsu and coauthors focused on the level of unpredictability in the players' decisions.[7] Economists call this "serial independence."

Serial independence means that the value of one item in a sequence is not affected by the value of another item in the sequence. In the case of tennis, serial independence means that the direction of a serve on one point should not affect the direction of a serve on the next point. People attempting to simulate randomness generally switch too often from one option to the other. A tennis player intent on remaining unpredictable might persistently alternate the direction in which he or she serves, and so actually become fairly predictable.[8]

The economists found that top tennis players closely approximate true randomness, confirming that tennis players' serve directions are governed by a mixed-strategy equilibrium. Note, however, that these studies of tennis look at the relatively simple decision of serving left or right. A recent study by economists who considered a wider set of options for servers and also analyzed the "muscle memory" advantages of hitting the same shot multiple times in a row show that tennis players don't fully optimize their serve strategies.[9] To truly maximize her chances of winning a point, a server would want to remain completely random. It seems that though she may not have a fully optimal strategy when all factors are considered, she comes close. Soccer and tennis thus demonstrate two elements of mixed-strategy equilibrium that are extremely important to a player who wishes to maximize her success: choosing the right probability of going in either direction, and doing so in a way that has no discernible pattern. For athletes with enough experience and incentive to get it right, these are skills that can be developed with practice.

For the rest of us, who play sports recreationally, getting the randomization and probabilities right is also useful if we want to win (and who doesn't?). But we are less likely to do it as effectively, because playing the right strategies and randomizing effectively both take practice. Luckily, your opponent doesn't have time to get it perfect either.

Wow, This Pitching Can Sure Get Complicated

Like tennis, baseball is one mixed-strategy game after another. Will the batter bunt? Will he fake a bunt and swing away, having drawn the third baseman out of position? Will the runner steal? If he does, will the pitcher throw a "pitchout" to catch him? Each of these decisions must be executed often enough to be useful but infrequently enough to be unpredictable. Beyond these many decisions, however, an even more frequent and elemental mixed-strategy game plays out in every baseball game. On every pitch, the pitcher must determine what pitch to throw, and the hitter must decide whether to swing. These choices present mixed strategies to both players. Like the penalty kick and tennis serve, every pitch in baseball requires both the pitcher and the hitter to make a decision that will maximize their outcome contingent on the other's decision, but without knowing what the other will do.

Suppose a batter has such a slow reaction time that he must decide before the pitch whether to swing or not. When I discussed the idea of a mixed strategy with my son David, he explained that he has a regular video game opponent who, when playing *MLB: The Show,* actually does decide whether to swing before the pitch. Knowing that his fairly incompetent friend has already chosen whether to swing, David purposely throws a lot more balls than most real pitchers do. Given that his friend's swing will occur independently of the quality of his pitch, David need not place the ball close to the strike zone if he expects a swing, and he should throw it right down the middle if he expects a take.

Of course, if David threw only balls, his friend would never swing and would walk continuously. But if David threw only strikes, his friend would swing every time and get a good number of hits. So David's goal is to throw just enough strikes that his friend continues to feel as though he should swing, but not enough that he allows many hits. As it turns out, this is a fairly easy equilibrium to reach and maintain against an unskilled opponent, and it yields a lot of swinging strikeouts. This situation almost perfectly parallels the soccer penalty kick situation and is much simpler than baseball pitching and swinging decisions faced by good players.

Before I get to mixed strategy in the major leagues, note that pitching situations exist in which mixed strategies do not apply. If a pitcher is so good at one pitch that he will always do best with that pitch, no matter what the hitter is expecting, then the pitcher will use that pitch exclusively. In that case, an economist would say that the best pitch is a "dominant strategy" in the same way that using steroids was a dominant strategy for Tour de France racers.

For example, when David played in the first few games of his final

Little League season, he and several of the other older kids could make every pitch a fastball down the middle. Most of the opposing batters could not catch up to it, and pitchers could be extremely effective with only a good fastball. But as the kids got better over the course of the season, David and the other kids had to learn to vary the speeds of their pitches and purposely throw out of the strike zone to keep batters off-balance. At a more advanced level, Mariano Rivera, the longtime closer for the Yankees, had such an effective cutter that he threw it almost exclusively—in one season, over 93 percent of the time. Batters knew it was coming but were usually helpless to do anything about it. Rivera thus did not have to be overly concerned with strategy. The former Red Sox starter Tim Wakefield came even closer to having a one-pitch dominant strategy. In 2008 he threw his knuckleball on 99.5 percent of his pitches.

Rivera and Wakefield were exceptions. The element of surprise is generally important in Major League Baseball and the equivalent international leagues. A professional hitter has about .27 seconds, by most estimates, to read the pitch location and allow it to inform his swing decision. That's not enough time to make a fully informed decision, so what the batter is expecting has a big influence on whether and how he swings. Because the pitcher knows the batter is reading and reacting to the pitch but has hardly any time to do so, the pitcher gains a large advantage if he fools the batter.

Rather than the two-option video game example, a major-league pitcher has several alternatives. New York Mets ace Jacob deGrom, for example, throws a fastball, a slider, and a changeup. When you add the options of various combinations of high, low, inside, outside, and in the strike zone, the set of pitches he can throw becomes extremely complicated. Other factors make pitcher and batter strategy still more difficult than the tennis or penalty kick examples. For one thing, pitcher and batter skill is highly idiosyncratic. Houston Astros ace Justin Verlander's fastball is much better than his breaking ball, and New York Yankees starter Corey Kluber's breaking ball is much better than his fastball. Verlander throws a lot more fastballs than Kluber, but they both mix things up to some degree (though one analysis showed Kluber should throw more breaking balls).[10] On top of that, some batters are much better at hitting fastballs than they are at hitting breaking balls. The legendary Oakland A's general manager Billy Beane, who was once a top pro prospect, apparently never stuck in the big leagues as a player because he couldn't hit a slider. If that story is true, then for any pitcher who had that pitch, throwing a slider was a dominant strategy when facing Beane.

Another factor that affects pitch strategy is the count. Pitchers should throw a fastball with a different probability—and batters should adjust their expectations accordingly—on the first pitch of an at-bat than on a count of three balls and one strike. A ball on the first pitch has a relatively low cost, but a ball on a three-and-one count puts a runner on base. Fastballs tend to be more accurate, so pitchers will throw them more often on three-and-one counts.

These and other factors make studying baseball pitch strategy more difficult than studying penalty kicks and the simple "serve left or right" studies of tennis. They also make it harder for baseball players to determine how often they should make each choice. In soccer, a kicker should kick right with almost exactly the same probability on pretty much every penalty kick; adjusting a bit for opponents (which is easy to do in tennis because you are playing one person for a hundred or more points), a tennis player should hit serves left or right at a constant probability throughout a match. But a pitcher should throw a fastball at a very different rate to Los Angeles Dodgers All-Star Mookie Betts on a three-and-one count with the bases loaded and one out late in a tie game (when a walk would be very costly) than on the first pitch of an at-bat to a mediocre hitter leading off the fourth inning with a three-run lead (when a single ball would have little consequence). Adding in differences in wind, temperature (it's harder to control pitches when it is cold), and stadium size, a pitcher needs not just Excel but a data science team to figure out how often to throw a fastball.

For more insight into these complexities, I talked to Matt Swartz, a Ph.D. economist and consultant for the Washington Nationals who has studied the game theory of pitching extensively.[11] "For the most part," he told me, "batters and pitchers follow mixed strategies pretty well." For example, R. A. Dickey was the most recent great knuckleball pitcher. Dickey also threw a few fastballs, and those fastballs were just as effective as those thrown by Justin Verlander, who (unlike Dickey) is often recognized for having one of the best fastballs in the game. Of course, if a batter knew a fastball was coming, he would typically do much better against Dickey. But Dickey used his fastball much less frequently. It was as effective as Verlander's because of the element of surprise, not its blazing speed.

But while Swartz finds that hitters and pitchers get the big picture right, there are details that they miss. Batters, he says, get "swing happy" when there are two strikes, and "pitchers don't take advantage of it enough." Pitchers, meanwhile, don't sufficiently adjust their strategies to their own strengths. "The league as a whole learns how often to throw each pitch in a given count. However, for example, if you are a great slider pitcher, you should throw a lot more sliders than other pitchers. But they don't, actually. They pitch like other pitchers." Overall, pitchers are very good at working out the mixed-strategy equilibrium. But as teams' analytics departments get better and better at using the troves of data now available, pitchers will likely get even better.

One implication of the intricacy of optimal pitch selection is that experience and intelligence are critical to pitching success. As Swartz puts it, "I would bet that Jamie Moyer had great mixed strategies."

Moyer, who was known for being crafty rather than particularly athletic, pitched in the major leagues until he was forty-seven years old.

Relative to pitchers, soccer players can more easily figure out optimal strategies when it comes to penalty kicks. But in more complex game-theoretic situations such as pitch selection, even pros who do the job for a living with millions of dollars on the line play the game less than optimally. Put another way, a supercomputer could not beat a soccer player in penalty kicks, but it could outsmart many pitchers or batters (if it first learned to pitch or hit).

This "supercomputer" effect in baseball has important implications for which player should decide which pitch should be thrown. Experience matters because, to call the ideal mix of pitches, a player needs to know a lot about the batter, the pitcher, the conditions that day, and the situation surrounding each at-bat. That's a lot of information to process. Who should do it? In the MLB, the catcher generally calls the pitches. The pitcher has a lot of influence as well, through pregame discussions with the catcher and by exercising veto power (pitchers often shake their heads in disapproval until the catcher calls the pitch the pitcher wants to throw). There may come a day when someone off the field with access to lots of data will call the pitches. But economics can't explain everything: it's possible that catchers and pitchers can make nuanced observations of their opponent's behavior at a given moment, and that additional information is more valuable than computing power.

Mike Matheny, who has been the manager of a few major-league teams after a career as a major-league catcher, thinks this on-field information trumps experience. He advises managers at all levels to let catchers call the pitches. "There is no way," he wrote on his blog, "that I could ever have a better sense of the game, or see the subtle things that only a catcher could see, from the dugout."[12] But Matheny also understands the value of experience in calling pitches, stressing the importance of teaching catchers how to understand each pitcher and "get the most out of them."

Other coaches and managers believe that experience trumps the value of the in-game information available to the catcher, and they therefore call the pitches from the dugout. This is especially true in high school and college baseball, where many catchers simply relay the coach's selections to the pitcher. Some anecdotal evidence suggests that coaches are becoming more active in calling pitches even at the higher levels of the sport, which would not be surprising, given baseball's increasing use of quantitative analysis. In any case, economics would predict that more experienced pitch callers are better at gathering all the relevant factors that determine the probability with which each pitch should be thrown and then randomizing properly among the options.

In the end, when it comes to pitching (unlike soccer penalty kicks), the optimal mixed strategy and randomization are sufficiently complex as to resist calculation in any useful time frame. In the case of pitch selection, both sides—the pitcher-catcher team and the hitter—are making incredibly complex decisions that combine conscious knowledge with intuition. The irony, and the beauty of the game, is that even if the pitcher and catcher make exactly the right call, and the pitcher executes the pitch perfectly, the batter sometimes gets a hit anyway.

Soccer, tennis, and baseball—not to mention Ping-Pong in the garage—all show us how game theory is important in sports, and how optimizing your strategy becomes increasingly difficult as the games grow more complicated. But those sports are far from the only places where knowledge of the mixed-strategy equilibrium is critical to excelling. Volleyball players fake spikes, football teams fake punts (though not as often as would be entertaining), and NASCAR drivers try to surprise their opponents about when and how they pass each other.

In each of these cases, success hinges on two things: knowing how often to employ each strategy, and randomizing among the strategies. To win, you have to be both smart and unpredictable.

6

How Does Discrimination Lead to a Proliferation of French Canadian Goalies?

"Integrating the NFL was the low point of my life," Woody Strode told *Sports Illustrated,* years after becoming the league's first Black player. "If I have to integrate heaven, I don't want to go."[1]

Although the story of Jackie Robinson is the most familiar tale of breaking barriers in sports, baseball was hardly the only American professional sports league to be tainted by segregation. The NFL fired all of its Black players in 1934; it was another twelve years before Strode and his teammate Kenny Washington returned racial diversity to the league.

For Strode and Washington, it was a matter of right place, right time. When the Rams moved from Cleveland to Los Angeles in 1946, the team wanted to play in Memorial Coliseum because it seated 100,000 people. Stadium administrators, supported by a crusading local sportswriter, demanded that the franchise sign a Black player. The Rams complied, turning to former UCLA teammates Washington and Strode.

The duo suffered the same sorts of taunting and cheap shots that Robinson did in his famous first season with the Dodgers a year later; like Robinson, they were also asked to stay in "racially appropriate" hotels when the team traveled. Washington, who saw more game action than Strode, was once held down by opponents at the bottom of a pile while they rubbed chalk in his eyes. "He could smile when his lip was bleeding," a college teammate said of him; in the NFL of 1946, he needed to. Within a couple of years, both he and Strode were out of the league, but other teams slowly signed Black players, and the NFL slowly accepted desegregation.

There was not a smooth, fairytale-like ascent from two Black NFL players in 1946 to today, when Black players make up nearly 70 percent of the league. It is nice to imagine that Strode and Washington and Robinson—and Chuck Cooper, Nat Clifton, and Earl Lloyd in the NBA in 1950; Lee Elder at the Masters golf tournament in 1975; Althea Gibson at Wimbledon in 1950; and Willie O'Ree in the NHL in 1958—made an immediate and lasting impact on their sports. To some degree, of course, they did; since World War II, no league has been resegregated after its color barrier was broken. But do athletes of color still face discrimination in less obvious ways? Economists have examined this question for decades, and they have found that the path to racial equality in sports has been bumpy and remains incomplete.

Overall, the story of discrimination in sports is uplifting. Social changes and market forces have helped many female and minority athletes. In economic terms, team owners learned that discrimination was a competitive disadvantage. The historical discrimination that came from fans, team owners, and the players themselves—which affected the racial makeup of teams, athletes' pay, and the positions and sports that were open to athletes—has been substantially reduced, and the explosive growth in sports revenue has been shared with an increasingly diverse athlete pool. Yet we still find discrimination in sports around the world. Markets often help correct injustice, but they can take a long time to do so.

Donald Sterling: Discrimination Poster Child

Economists like to classify discrimination as one of two kinds: either taste based or statistical. The poster child for taste-based discrimination is the former Los Angeles Clippers owner Donald Sterling, who was recorded saying to his mistress, "Why are you taking pictures with minorities? Why? It's like talking to an enemy. . . . It bothers me a lot that you're associating with black people. . . . You don't have to have yourself walking with black people."[2] Sterling's words implied a "distaste" for people of color that almost certainly made him less likely to employ them relative to a comparable white person.

Statistical discrimination, on the other hand, is usually practiced by employers and others who want to sort a large pool of people based on empirically supported stereotypes. For instance, a warehouse foreman might interview more men than women for an open position moving refrigerators because men are stronger, on average, than women. Of course, any one woman might be stronger than any one man, but on a large scale, the foreman's discriminatory behavior has a statistical foundation. Just because it makes mathematical sense, however, doesn't mean statistical discrimination is legally or morally acceptable. For example, a woman qualified to move refrigerators would have a compelling legal and moral case against a foreman who passed her over for a similarly qualified man.[3]

Taste-based discrimination, not statistical discrimination, dominates the injustices seen in sports. In the decades after Jackie Robinson's debut, study after study showed that across a number of major sports, white players received preferential treatment compared with Black players. It is not always clear exactly who is discriminating, however, as taste-based discrimination can generally come from at least three sources (and, in the case of sports, a fourth).

First, we have Donald Sterling–style *employer* discrimination, in which the people in charge of hiring prefer one demographic group over another. Employers can also practice statistical discrimination, as in the refrigerator-moving example. But the distinction between the two is that a statistically discriminating foreman who brought in more men to interview would happily hire a woman if she proved herself to be the strongest candidate. For a taste-based discriminating foreman, a woman would need to be substantially more productive than a man (or willing to work at a much lower wage) to be considered for the job, because she would need to compensate for the foreman's aversion to working with women.

Second, taste-based discrimination can take the form of *employee* discrimination, in which workers from an in-group don't want to work with workers from an out-group. For example, consider a perfectly nondiscriminating manager in charge of hiring workers for a relatively low-level position at the Lahore Lions cricket team's office in Pakistan. Suppose the more specialized team management positions are already staffed by Sunni Muslims who have a "distaste" for Shia Muslims. Faced with two equally qualified candidates, one Sunni and one Shia, the completely unbiased manager has a strong incentive to hire the Sunni candidate. That manager is aware that if the Shia candidate gets the job, discriminating Sunnis, who make up the entire active workforce, will make the new employee's life unpleasant and may work less efficiently. So the manager might choose the Sunni candidate to keep other employees happy even though doing so is, in the bigger picture, unfair and wrong.

Third, taste-based discrimination can take the form of *customer* discrimination. In markets where a substantial portion of the customer base discriminates, a business focused solely on profits might argue that it is forced to discriminate. Consider the owner of professional hockey's Montreal Canadiens. A majority of the team's fan base speaks French, making it the only fan base in the league that isn't primarily English speaking. Meanwhile the league's labor force—its players—includes plenty of French Canadians. Regardless of whether the owner cares about players' native tongues, customers will probably prefer that the players speak French, so the owner might be tempted, due to higher profits, to discriminate in favor of French speakers and against English, Russian, and Swedish speakers.

The final form of discrimination, and the one largely specific to sports, is referee discrimination. If all of the officials in a sport are white and favor others of their race, fielding a white team could have advantages in terms of getting favorable calls. The economists Joseph Price and Justin Wolfers have shown that NBA referees are more lenient to players of their own race, such that the composition of a referee squad likely affects the outcome of many NBA games. And historically, NBA referees and officials in other sports have been disproportionately white, which could, on balance, have led to a disadvantage for minority players.[4]

Who Is Racist: Fans or Front Offices?

The Minnesota Timberwolves' 2012–2013 season was not especially memorable, though the team's thirty-one wins (against fifty-one losses) were, depressingly enough, its most in six years. Those Timberwolves, however, will leave a lasting legacy not for their on-court performance but for the composition of their roster. Not since Larry Bird's Celtics teams of the 1980s had an NBA franchise fielded as many white players as that year's Wolves, who rostered white guys ranging from superstar forward Kevin Love to Montenegrin big man Nikola Pekovic to redheaded former volleyball standout Chase Budinger.[5] In a league that was 78 percent Black, the Timberwolves were two-thirds white. If you had distributed all of that season's NBA players at random among the teams, the odds of having one team end up with ten white and five Black players were one in ten thousand.

Confronted by reporters, the Minnesota front office denied that the team's racial makeup was at all intentional. But few thought it a coincidence that the Timberwolves play in the NBA's whitest market, and one with an ugly history of taste-based discrimination by its sports team owners. Calvin Griffith, the owner of baseball's Washington Senators, moved the team to Minneapolis in 1961 and renamed it the Minnesota Twins. In 1978, Griffith told a crowd at a local Lions Club event that he had chosen to relocate there "when I found out you only had 15,000 blacks here. . . . We came here because you've got good, hardworking, white people here."[6] Griffith, a holdover from the pre–Jackie Robinson era when, as the journalist and podcaster Josh Levin put it, "owners hated Black people more than they liked money," moved his team from a city with a majority Black population to a smaller and potentially less lucrative market to keep his fan base white.[7]

The Timberwolves, denying any preference for players of a certain color, claimed that the team's demographic makeup was a consequence of the organization's global scouting efforts, which had hauled in five international players, all white, to the opening-day roster. And, admittedly, nobody knows for sure whether the Wolves were going out of their way to sign white players. The team did become slightly less white by the 2013–2014 season's opening night. But it was by no means unreasonable for civil rights activists to call attention to the roster's skewed racial makeup; the Wolves' whiteness was unprecedented by recent NBA standards.

Implied in these allegations was a charge that the Timberwolves were suffering from employer discrimination, customer discrimination, or both. If the whitewashing was deliberate, then either Minnesota fans were demanding a whiter team and ownership was responding, or ownership simply preferred white players. This phenomenon appears to have haunted the league on a larger scale for decades.

The NBA offers a microcosm of larger patterns of discrimination in the United States. After the NBA was integrated in 1950, a legion of Black stars quickly inundated the league. By 1965, six of the ten All-Star Game starters were Black; in 1975, the first year in which fans voted for the All-Star team, four of the five leading vote getters were Black. Between 1954 and 1970, the Black share of the league's labor force shot from 4.6 percent to 54.3 percent.[8]

But all was not well for the increasingly dominant Black group of players. A raft of studies, including ones by the economists Gerald Scully and Lawrence Kahn, showed a long-standing pattern of wage discrimination: Black NBA players significantly outperformed white ones at equivalent pay levels, and Black players were more likely to be cut from teams than equally good white players.[9] Put differently, a Black basketball player in 1985 had to score more points or grab more rebounds than his white teammate to make the same salary or keep his job.

Were all thirty NBA ownership groups colluding to underpay Black players in a blatantly racist conspiracy? Not necessarily. It's certainly possible that some NBA owners in 1985 held a distaste for Black people—Sterling bought the Clippers in 1981—but they were also likely responding to the racist preferences of their fan bases. Several economic studies, while varying slightly in their specifics, found that fans in the 1980s were more likely to attend basketball games if more of the home team's players were white.[10] Researchers also found that white players were not evenly distributed across teams but clustered in markets with more white fans. So even if the fans didn't actually discriminate, the league's general managers assembled their teams as if fans did, valuing the white players more in cities with larger white fan bases. White players were concentrated in white cities: Bill Walton played in Portland; John Stockton played in Utah; Larry Bird, Kevin McHale, John Havlicek, and Dave Cowens all played in notoriously racist Boston; and so on.

But attitudes about race have changed. Although racism is both casually and empirically observable in the present-day United States, it was more overt a few decades ago. Americans' approval of interracial marriages, for example, has trended in roughly linear fashion from 4 percent in 1958 to nearly 90 percent in recent years.[11] As the social structures and ways of thinking left over from segregation fade away, logic suggests that discrimination in the NBA will recede as well. And for the most part, it has. A number of economists reexamined the data for seasons in the 1990s, and most found little evidence of salary discrimination. By the mid-1990s, Black players were earning roughly as much as comparably skilled white players. The same was true for the findings on exit discrimination.[12]

Present-day studies have concluded that wage discrimination no longer exists in the NBA. I don't know of any formal tests of whether fans still have discriminatory tastes, but a crude survey of recent opening-day rosters showed no correlation between the whiteness of a team's fan base and its players. In various years, the Warriors, Bucks, Grizzlies, Lakers, and Spurs have been among the teams with the highest proportions of white players—but the composition of their home cities has been diverse, ranging from predominantly white (Milwaukee) to substantially Latino (Los Angeles and San Antonio) or Asian (San Francisco–Oakland) to the most heavily Black city in the league (Memphis).

This trend reflects one of the pillars of the Nobel Prize–winning economist Gary Becker's theory of discrimination. Becker hypothesized that markets correct for discrimination: firms that are less willing to hire minorities will ultimately be driven out of business by firms that hire based only on talent. As teams realized that ignoring or underpaying Black players would harm them in the win-loss column more than it would help attract prejudiced fans, teams ceased to discriminate. In other words, winning mattered more to fans—and thus to teams' bottom lines—than the racial makeup of their rosters. Even Sterling's Clippers had only one white player under contract in 2013–2014. The fading of discrimination reflected the change in underlying social attitudes. If fans had remained as prejudiced as they were in 1970, a wise owner would have given up a few wins to have more white players. But as fans became more open-minded, it became increasingly costly for owners who were prejudiced to indulge their own discrimination. Overall, competition helped raise the pay and job security of Black players.

The huge increase in athletes' salaries has also raised the cost of discriminating. Other settings (for example, police forces of one race policing cities dominated by another race) often have no competitive marketplace to drive out discrimination. So, while good evidence suggests that competition and economics erode discrimination, Becker's theory can be misused to justify government inaction in the face of discrimination. But at least in some leagues, money and winning come first, and that's good for talented athletes from historically underrepresented groups.

As for the Timberwolves, probably due to some combination of competitive forces and negative publicity associated with their unusually white roster, the team quickly began to look more like the rest of the league. The team had a 62 percent Black roster by 2015–2016 and had even surpassed the league average with an 80 percent Black roster in 2020–2021.

The Timberwolves' racial makeup may well have held the team back, but it was not the only factor, as the team has continued to stink after adding Black players to the roster. While we don't have strong evidence that racial composition hurt the Timberwolves, the economist Stefan Symanski showed, using a broad data set from English professional soccer, that "teams with a below-average proportion of black players have tended to achieve inferior playing performance."[13] So, though the Timberwolves' example suggests that nonprejudicial behavior of owners is not sufficient to field a winner in the extremely competitive world of modern professional sports, the data in soccer and elsewhere suggest that nonprejudicial team formation is necessary to remain competitive.

Race-Free Discrimination in Hockey

Let's move to a sport where you might not expect discrimination to be relevant: professional hockey, where a mere 2 or 3 percent of players are nonwhite. Black players in the National Hockey League are sometimes subject to shamefully inappropriate taunting and slurs.[14] But largely because of the small sample size, we have little research or empirical evidence to suggest that they face economic discrimination.

The NHL's near racial homogeneity doesn't mean that it has avoided a somewhat storied history of questionable hiring practices. The NHL may be America's whitest major sports league, but it is certainly international, with substantial numbers of English Canadian, French Canadian, American, Czech, Finnish, Swedish, Russian, and Slovakian players. Most research on discrimination in the NHL, however, has been confined to the pay gap between the league's two biggest demographic groups: French Canadians and English Canadians.

Relations between minority French Canadians and the rest of Canada have often been frosty. The low point occurred in 1969 and 1970, with the bombing of the Montreal Stock Exchange and the murder of a government official by separatist French Canadian terrorists. Although those tragedies were anomalous in their magnitude, language policies in Quebec, Canada's lone French-speaking province, continue to generate controversy. Many residents of Quebec still dream of independence.[15]

The earliest credible study of discrimination in the NHL, published in 1987 by three Canadian economists, found that French Canadian players as a group tended to outperform English Canadian players as a group.[16] Like the similar research in the NBA, this study operated on the assumption that if one demographic group was routinely outperforming another, a player from the high-performing minority group (in this case French Canadians) must have had to meet a higher standard than the lower-performing majority group (in this case English Canadians) to gain a spot on the team.

The study also computed performance differentials by position. It showed that defensemen apparently faced the most hiring discrimination, while forwards faced less, and goalies seemed to face none at all. The authors proposed a clever and sensible explanation for this gap: positions for which performance is more easily measured are less subject to discrimination, while positions that require more subjective evaluation suffer from greater discrimination. Forwards' play can be measured by the number of goals and assists they produce, while defensemen's impact on the game involves historically less measurable abilities like checking, passing, and situational awareness. It's easier for a team to select against French Canadian defensemen than French Canadian forwards because it's harder (or at least it was, before the sports analytics trend hit hockey in recent years) to make a concrete case that one defenseman is better than another.

Goalies have an obvious performance metric in save percentage. They also are more isolated from the rest of the team than the other players, which likely reduces employee (teammate) discrimination on the basis of language. Consequently, French Canadian goalies seem to avoid discrimination altogether.

The study made a fairly convincing argument that the market is better at driving out racism when performance can be measured more easily. Scouts evaluating forwards can put aside any preconceived notions they have, knowing that it will cost the team too much to pass over a French-speaking player who scores more. But the same team's coach can tell himself he is choosing the defenseman who speaks his language because he's a tougher or more savvy player, and there is no easy way for anyone to show the coach was wrong. To borrow from psychology, "confirmation bias"—talking yourself into believing what you want to be true—is stronger when the data are more subjective.

To analogize to the business world, an economist would expect to find that discrimination gets driven out by the market in sales or financial-analyst jobs, where performance is relatively easily measured, but maybe not in some middle-manager positions, where performance can be measured very subjectively.[17] Along the same lines, referees subjectively evaluate players all the time, and as noted earlier, a study showed that NBA referees favor players of their own race. Those findings received front-page coverage in the *New York Times,* putting public relations pressure on the NBA.[18] Since the story was published, the NBA has invested substantial resources in measuring and standardizing referees' calls. By scrutinizing refereeing and adding reviews to make it more objectively measurable, the NBA has, according to more recent research, eradicated the bias in refereeing.[19]

Where Are All the Black Pitchers?

Quick, name a recent African American pitcher besides Cy Young Award winners C. C. Sabathia and David Price.[20] Marcus Stroman? Chris Archer? Chances are you couldn't come up with many names; hardly any players in baseball fit the description. Although African Americans have typically accounted for at least 25 percent of major-league outfielders, they have never made up more than 10 percent of pitchers or catchers. In recent years, a mere handful of African American pitchers, and not a single African American catcher, have appeared on major-league rosters.[21]

What causes this positional segregation? No one has a definitive answer. The first of two primary theories attributes the lack of African American pitchers and catchers to systemic racism among coaches, scouts, and general managers, who may believe Black people lack the leadership and thinking skills necessary to play pitcher and catcher, and therefore don't train them for these positions; or at the higher levels, managers shift Black players to positions they see as requiring less intelligence. Widespread evidence of racist stereotyping against the intelligence of Black people is available both empirically and anecdotally. Polling done by the University of Chicago's General Social Survey routinely finds that respondents rate white people's intelligence higher than Black people's.[22] In the baseball world, Al Campanis, the white general manager of the Los Angeles Dodgers, made headlines in the 1980s (and was forced to resign) after he told the news anchor Ted Koppel that he thought Black people "may not have some of the necessities to be, let's say, a field manager, or, perhaps, a general manager."[23] Given that Campanis had been a general manager for nineteen years, his comment led many to wonder how pervasive such views were in baseball generally. Campanis was not alone. Cincinnati Reds owner Marge Schott was repeatedly suspended for using racist slurs and allegedly saying things too vile to paraphrase here.[24]

Other peripheral facts strengthen the case that prejudice plays a substantial role in positional segregation. For one thing, Japanese players in Major League Baseball are disproportionately represented at pitcher. Given the common American stereotype of Asians as especially smart, their increased presence at pitcher supports the stereotype argument, since executives seem to think pitcher is a higher-intelligence position.

This apparent prejudice among scouts, coaches of young players, and voters for the Cy Young Award exemplifies statistical discrimination. These parties may have no conscious animus or ill will toward African Americans. But if a coach believes that African Americans are less intelligent, he will direct young African Americans away from pitching or catching. The racist coach may think he is acting in the prospect's best interests by matching him to a position appropriate for his mental capacity. Here the distinction between taste-based and statistical discrimination is meaningless because the player is given no chance to prove he can be an effective pitcher.

As beliefs evolve over time, positional discrimination should be corrected by the market. For instance, the recent advances of African American quarterbacks in the NFL may suggest that statistical discrimination at that position is waning. As Marc Morial, president and CEO of the National Urban League, recently wrote, "For decades, the prevailing view seemed to be that while African Americans made good runners, blockers and receivers, they did not possess the ability or intellect to be quarterback."[25] But things can change (though it can take a long time): the *New Yorker* declared 2014 "the Year of the Black Quarterback."[26] In the five seasons after that article was published, three NFL Most Valuable Player Awards were bestowed on Black quarterbacks. Before that, Black players had made inroads at middle linebacker and center, both of which are leadership and strategic positions that have historically been dominated by white players.[27]

In addition to misguided statistical discrimination, another economics-based explanation for positional segregation exists. Proponents of this argument believe that pitcher and catcher are more specialized positions than infielder or outfielder. Pitchers require more focused training and instruction, and catchers need not only training but also fairly expensive equipment. African Americans, who have higher poverty rates than any other ethnic group except American Indians, are less likely to have access to the instructional tools and coaches that are key to developing pitching and catching (and quarterbacking) skills. This theory is generally supported by participation rates of Black people in the sports landscape as a whole. They are heavily represented in basketball and, to a lesser extent, soccer—sports that require little equipment—while Black players are less prevalent in sports that require a good deal of equipment or facility access, like golf, hockey, and swimming. Structural racism still drives athletic outcomes to a substantial degree.

The jury is still out on which of these two explanations better explains positional segregation. Clear correlation exists between the costs of a sport and the proportion of players from underrepresented groups. On the other hand, quarterbacks don't need more specialized equipment than wide receivers. It seems likely that stereotypes and resource differences have both contributed to segregating certain sports and positions.

Gender and Prize Money

It's no secret that men dominate the mainstream sports scene. For example, a quick comparison of the NBA and WNBA attendance records demonstrates which league currently generates greater fan interest. Does the fact that the *minimum* NBA salary is more than seven times as high as the *maximum* WNBA salary constitute discrimination? Discrimination could be part of the difference, but the difference in itself is not evidence of discrimination.

Even the Women's Sports Foundation abstains from advocating equal salaries across gender lines for sports like basketball. Women's basketball leagues just do not draw as much interest as men's basketball leagues and therefore cannot raise the revenue necessary to compensate their players as well as the men. In economics terms, the WNBA's product (the games) attracts less demand (fewer fans), keeping the league's profits well below those of the prosperous NBA. One can certainly argue about the cause of the disparity: some fans would say men's basketball is simply more entertaining, while others would argue that women's basketball is in the process of establishing a fan base and brand just as the NBA did decades earlier. This second argument would reflect some version of taste-based customer discrimination. Regardless, most women's professional sports leagues are governed by the same facts: they have fewer fans than the men's equivalent, and their players receive much lower salaries. Even if progressively minded WNBA owners wanted to pay their players NBA-level salaries, they would quickly go bankrupt if they tried.

By contrast, one sport where women have a good case for discrimination is one where they are paid very well: tennis. Indeed, in terms of pay, tennis is the dominant women's sport. It draws the highest ratings and biggest crowds, and its players make the most in both tournament winnings and endorsement money. According to *Forbes* magazine, the nine highest-paid female athletes in the world in 2020 were all tennis players (soccer star Alex Morgan ranked tenth).[28] Whereas all-time women's basketball greats like A'ja Wilson and Breanna Stewart may not be familiar to the average observer, most casual sports fans can name at least a handful of top active women's tennis players at any given time.

The biggest tennis tournaments are run by the same governing body for men and women. The four Grand Slam events—the U.S., Australian, and French Opens and Wimbledon—are conducted simultaneously for both genders, with equal-sized 128-player fields. In tennis tournaments hosted at the same venue by the same organizer, at which tickets earn admission to both draws, it's nearly impossible to parse out interest in the men's event from the women's. The women might, at least theoretically, generate half the revenue, so it would certainly seem like outright discrimination to award them less prize money.

It took until 1973 before any Grand Slam event seriously considered equalizing its prize money. In that year, women's players at the U.S. Open threatened to strike if they were not compensated equally to men. The tournament's organizers acquiesced to the demand, and the U.S. Open has awarded equal purses to men and women ever since. The Australian and French Opens soon followed suit. It took until 2007, however, for the last holdout, Wimbledon, to finally raise the women's purse to equal the men's. Until that time, the All England Lawn Tennis and Croquet Club continued to distribute more money to the men than to the women in the same tournament. Was Wimbledon discriminating?

For Wimbledon's behavior to have been justified, the event's organizers would have needed evidence that the men's tournament drew a greater share of the revenue than the women's tournament. But such evidence is hard to come by. Television ratings were far more difficult to access in the 1970s and 1980s than they are today, but one economist quotes a CBS executive in the mid-1970s as saying the women's tournament actually drew larger viewing audiences than the men's. For that study, the economist also obtained Nielsen ratings for the 1988 Wimbledon finals, which showed that the women drew a substantially larger share than the men. Interpreting ratings is complicated, though, given that men play best-three-out-of-five-sets matches, while women play best two out of three, so men's matches typically have more commercial breaks, which generate revenue.[29]

If these results held even somewhat true for all the years between 1973 and 2007, then women's tennis players would probably have done well to unionize and sue Wimbledon. If the body that oversees major tennis championships were more subject to competitive pressures, the women would probably have done better sooner.

Now that Grand Slam purses are equal by gender, is discrimination gone from tennis? Maybe in terms of prize money at Grand Slam events. But even though tennis players are the highest-paid female athletes, the top women make noticeably less than the best-paid men. *Tennis* magazine reported the following after the 2018 U.S. Open: "The women's final attracted 3,101,000 viewers, while the men's final between Novak Djokovic and Juan Martin del Potro drew in 2,065,000 viewers."[30] In that same year, four male tennis players and no women made *Forbes*'s list of highest-paid athletes.

Market forces have been a valuable weapon for reducing discriminatory treatment of women and minorities in sports, and in labor markets more broadly. But there are limits. If customers are prejudiced, historically underrepresented groups will remain at a disadvantage. Eliminating that sort of discrimination requires social, not economic, change. At other times, no competitive pressure exists (such as when all MLB or NFL owners agreed to have white-only leagues; or when Wimbledon, being such a dominant tennis institution, could do whatever it wanted), and thus no market incentive for things to change. But the other limit—and maybe the greatest enemy of fairness—is that when animus is deep and widespread, markets can be painfully slow to help those on the wrong side of discrimination. Minorities and women have come a long way in the U.S. labor market, thanks in part to market forces and competition. But economists have shown quite clearly that civil rights laws were essential in creating and sustaining momentum for women and minorities in the U.S. labor market when market forces were moving much too slowly.[31] Economics is powerful, but intolerance and stereotypes are strong competitors.

7

How Do Ticket Scalpers
Make the World a Better Place?

In 2001, Amy Stephens was a middle-school teacher in the Atlanta suburbs. One weekend she took a trip to New York with her husband. The couple planned ahead and bought tickets to *The Producers,* a very hot Broadway musical at the time. But a family complication arose, and Amy opted to sell the tickets rather than go to the show. That simple decision changed her life forever. "We bought the two tickets for a hundred bucks, sold them on eBay for five hundred, and there it came. I was like, 'Wow, that was easy.'"[1] Amy didn't know it yet, but she was on her path to becoming a full-time professional ticket scalper.

When they returned to Atlanta, Amy and her husband started "picking up tickets here and there, then throwing them on eBay." They still had no plans to make this more than a sideline, but things changed a year after the New York trip, when Amy had her first child. She had been planning to take a long maternity leave anyway, and she and her husband realized she could make money at the same time by expanding the ticket resale venture. She has been running Amy's Tickets ever since. "It happened by accident," she says, "but it became a huge source of income."

From the start, Amy's business was built on a simple system. She bought tickets from college and pro teams when they became available, and later offered them through eBay. "We buy season tickets to good college teams, and we have contracts with arenas—I get first right of refusal for certain seats for every event there. These places work with brokers to shift inventory."

The teams whose tickets Amy sold didn't necessarily like her; they would have preferred to get the extra money she was making as profit. But they tolerated her because she could reach fans that they couldn't, and she could vary her prices in ways the teams could not. The priority for teams—especially college teams—was simply to sell bunches of season tickets. They were happy to leave to Amy the work of breaking them up and finding buyers for each game. She was equally happy to be the profiting middlewoman.

Things couldn't have been running more smoothly or profitably. "It used to be that, anything I tried to sell, I made money hand over fist," she recalls.

A few years after she got her eBay-based business up and running, Amy evolved it further with the help of a new entrant into the ticket marketplace: StubHub. Initially, the new site seemed to make her system work even better; it took care of customer service issues, and it attracted fans in hordes.

Yet what StubHub giveth, StubHub taketh away. After several years of making her business bigger and better, StubHub shifted its focus and became far less kind to Amy.

When Amy started her business in 2001, StubHub was still a fledgling start-up. But by 2014, StubHub was the first place most fans would go to buy and sell tickets. As it developed its technology to make directly transferring tickets easier and easier, and as buyers and sellers became comfortable with StubHub as a middleman, Amy wasn't needed as much. As she put it to me in 2014, "StubHub has been our partner, but they are getting to be our competitor. . . . I doubt there's a future in selling twenty or thirty season tickets for a college football team. We have built our lives on this business, and I don't know what the future holds." Yet even as StubHub is making the newly democratized ticket business more difficult for small resellers, it faces pressures of its own. Teams, event planners, and even speculators are trying to take back the market from the people.

The Evolution of the Ticket Market I: The Past

One of the first recorded uses of tickets was for events at the Roman Colosseum—gladiator contests, chariot races, and the like. Seats were assigned; pottery shards served as indicators of where to sit. Although entry was free, demand for seats was often huge, so people had to line up for tickets. Citizens of higher class got preferential treatment and seating. We have no surviving record of ticket resale in that era.[2]

Sometime in the intervening centuries, the people who organized sporting events began to see tickets as a source of profit, which led to the first big change: tickets started to cost money. (Also at some point, the pottery shards were replaced by paper tickets; paper reached the Arab world in the eighth century A.D. and Europe in the eleventh.) Fans began to take it for granted that if enough people wanted to see a sporting event, they would be charged. But for a long while, sporting events did not have *advance* ticket sales.

This trend was broken in Renaissance times. Sixteenth-century English theater operators are the first group documented to have sold tickets at different prices and to allocate better places to people willing to pay more. They also realized that when tickets were scarce, it was useful to give patrons a chance to plan ahead.[3] For their most hotly anticipated events, they forged an additional innovation: they introduced advance sales, to allocate tickets through a combination of time and money.

Over the centuries, advance ticket sales became more common, and at some point they gave birth to the ticket resale business. Although people liked the opportunity to buy in advance, plans sometimes changed. People bought tickets to games and then found they couldn't go, or decided shortly before a sold-out big game that they wanted to attend and needed a way to get in.

Enter ticket brokers—and, as a subset of them are less affectionately known, scalpers. Economists *love* scalpers, or at least one primary aspect of scalping. Ticket resale creates what economists call "gains from trade." Suppose you had tickets to an NFL game, but your daughter's soccer team made the playoffs, and her game created a conflict. The football tickets would now be worth less to you than they were when you had originally planned to attend the game. By selling your tickets to someone who valued them more, you could make some money and also make the world a marginally happier place. If you valued the ticket price at zero once you decided to go to your daughter's game, and someone out there was willing to pay $100 for it, then you could sell the ticket to that person for anything less than $100 and make you *both* better off. You get some money instead of a ticket that would go to waste, and the other guy gets a ticket for less than what he was willing to pay for it. It's a win-win.

Although that's a nice story, it wasn't always so easy to get to the happy ending. In the days before StubHub, it was hard for someone with an extra ticket to find someone else who wanted it. That's where scalpers and ticket brokers came in. Once your daughter's game was scheduled, you could take your ticket down to (the imaginary) Vinny's Ticket Shop at the local shopping center. You could sell Vinny your ticket for $50, and the guy who was willing to pay up to $100 could come in and buy it from Vinny for $80. You and the new buyer could have done better if you had found each other independently of Vinny and you sold him the ticket for, say, $60. But in pre-internet times, that transaction was usually either impossible or so time-consuming to set up that the money you made was not worth the hours you put into it. So the broker—or, if you prefer, scalper—was valuable: Vinny's presence made you, the guy who ultimately bought the ticket, and Vinny himself all better off.

In pre-internet times, scalpers and brokers also provided another valuable service: they acted as simple distributors. Depending on where you lived, a trip to the stadium box office could be inconvenient. If Vinny went to the box office, bought a bunch of tickets, and sold them in the neighborhood of Vinny's Ticket Shop, everyone was better off. Just as Walmart provides a service by selling soap so that you don't have to go to Cincinnati to buy it directly from Procter and Gamble, Vinny provided a valuable service by cutting down travel and wait times.

Although economists love ticket scalpers, lots of other people hate them. If you type "ticket scalpers" into Google's search bar, the auto-fill engine comes up with entries like "ticket scalpers are bad actors" and "fans hate being gouged by ticket scalpers." Ticket brokers don't get as bad a rap—the distinction being that scalpers operate outside arenas at game time, and brokers buy and sell tickets leading up to the game—but they rarely get a lot of praise.

One simple driver of scalpers' bad reputation is bad experiences. As Chris Tsakalakis, former president of StubHub, told me, "Anyone who ever paid more than face value for a ticket doesn't believe in economics, and anyone who ever received less than face value for a ticket doesn't believe in economics." In other words, people used to get indignant (and often took their anger out on scalpers) when they felt they paid too much as buyers or got too little as sellers. They were not the ones getting a good deal; the scalpers were.

Another downside of doing business with ticket resellers was the possibility of outright fraud. Some scalpers, it's true, sold counterfeit tickets. If a scalper sold you a ticket in front of the arena and the ticket turned out to be a fake, you were very unlikely to get your money back. Outright dishonesty is indeed a bad thing. But we have little evidence to suggest that fake tickets ever posed such a problem that counterfeiting alone should have shut down the secondary market.

Another reason people were wary of brokers and scalpers was the belief that scalpers often bought up all the tickets to a game and drove up the resale price. This scenario could theoretically lead to seats sitting empty despite there being people who would have occupied them if the tickets were reasonably priced. But while fans and teams regularly accuse scalpers and brokers of trying to corner the market, essentially no evidence indicates that they have ever tried—at least not at games with a large capacity. At a baseball or football game with forty thousand seats, a group of scalpers would have to buy thousands of tickets to corner the market, a feat for which they likely lack both the opportunity and the resources. I don't know of a single documented example of market domination by scalpers.

In their heyday, the biggest argument against scalpers and brokers was probably that they wasted time and resources. For any given fan, a scalper might save that person the time of standing in line. But, as a group, scalpers made it harder for fans to get access directly to tickets when they became available, and forced fans to search around before eventually finding the scalper. If fans could have bought and sold without a middleman, presumably they could have kept more of the money, and the potential scalpers and brokers could have done something more productive with their lives.

Consider the buildup to the Boston Bruins' appearance in the 2011 Stanley Cup Finals, their first in more than twenty years. On the night before the team box office put tickets up for sale, hundreds of fans camped out in line; when the box office opened the next day, the games sold out in minutes.

But a lot of the buyers weren't fans at all. Many of them walked directly across the street to a row of ticket broker offices to sell their tickets for a profit.[4] These resellers' decision to camp out for tickets that would have sold out either way wasted the time of everybody in line by creating a longer wait. One economic analysis of rock concert tickets (a market very similar to sports tickets) showed that the effect of resellers in the early arrival game was truly costly, in the sense that they wasted a lot of people's time.[5]

Overall, ticket brokers did hurt fans who regularly bought tickets early. But those costs were more than offset by the gains brokers provided to fans who wanted to buy tickets closer to game day, avoid the trouble of waiting in line, or easily sell tickets if their plans changed. So while a few fans—those who waited extra long in ticket release lines or accidentally bought counterfeit tickets—had good cause to dislike ticket resellers, the antiscalper vitriol was unwarranted for the vast majority of ticket buyers.

Like fans, teams have also historically opposed scalping. From a selfish perspective, this attitude is perfectly understandable. For one thing, when demand for a game was low, resellers could purchase tickets below face value from season ticket holders and fans who found out they could not attend a game after prepurchasing tickets. If they resold these tickets to other fans below face value, that discount hurt a team's reputation and encouraged fans not to bother purchasing tickets directly from the team. They could just wait until they found tickets below face value, which, in turn, discouraged people from buying season tickets at full price in the first place.

But the main reason teams hated scalpers is that the teams wanted to be more like airlines. Although airplane tickets and sports tickets are in most ways similar, airlines have a big advantage that teams do not: their tickets cannot be resold. A person who buys a flight ticket has to show identification to prove that she is the one entitled to use it. Thus, as the date of a flight approaches, the price of an airline ticket goes up, often dramatically. Prices are higher, sometimes a lot higher, for flights that leave tomorrow than for those that leave in a week; flights that leave next week are, in turn, more expensive than those that leave in a few months.

For sports, these trends are inverted. The economist Andrew Sweeting crunched the numbers for baseball ticket sales on eBay and found that a ticket that sold for $50 two months before a game was worth about $38, on average, a week before the game, and $30 on game day.[6] Unsurprisingly, the game-approaching discount is much greater for tickets sold by individuals—those who are just trying to get rid of tickets they can't use, and by game day will often give them away for free—than for brokers.

Ticket brokers undermined teams' pricing power by buying tickets at the advance purchase price and undercutting their desire to raise prices as the event neared. A team couldn't charge a lot for a last-minute ticket when a scalper in the parking lot was offering a lower price. But while teams have always hated scalpers for this reason, fans should love them for it. They create competition in the market, and for buyers, more competition among sellers is always better.

In any case, until recently, sports teams disliked brokers and scalpers, but apparently not enough to get rid of them. Remember, it's easy to get rid of ticket resale if you sell tickets only at the door, just before the event. Teams tolerated brokers as a side effect of advance sales.

The Evolution of the Market II: The Present

This tenuous relationship of grudging tolerance among fans, teams, and scalpers continued unchanged for pretty much the entire second half of the twentieth century. But the internet transformed the industry. The arrival of sites like StubHub put significant pressure on brokers like Amy's Tickets, since people with extra tickets could now easily find people who wanted to buy them.

How did StubHub's entry change brokers' and scalpers' business models? First, StubHub tore down the barriers to entry for people who wanted to enter the ticket resale business. Ticket brokers once needed to invest in storefronts, or at least spend money developing and marketing their websites. But "how to become a ticket broker" articles now abound on the internet, and most of them suggest operating as a StubHub super-user. This may be the one promise that you can get into a business opportunity with "no money down!" that is actually true. But this ease of entry makes competition fierce, so new entrants are likely to have trouble earning much of a living.

A second effect of StubHub is that it has made the secondary market for tickets much "thicker"; that is, a lot more tickets are being offered for sale, all on a single site. This has put serious pressure on ticket resellers' margins. More tickets are great if you're looking to buy, but not so much if you're the seller.

A third downside for brokers is that they are getting cut out: consumers now buy and sell on StubHub without middlemen. According to one estimate, 60 percent of StubHub sales in the company's early days were made through brokers, but a few years later, 60 percent were direct sales from one fan to another.[7] A scalper summed up the situation succinctly to a *New York Times* reporter: "StubHub is killing us."[8]

Finally, StubHub has trained consumers to be smarter. The pattern of resale prices dropping as a game approaches wasn't a problem for brokers and scalpers when they could count on selling tickets at high prices way in advance to fans who didn't want to risk getting shut out of a game. But many of those fans have now figured out that, thanks to StubHub, tickets will still be widely available in the days leading up to the game.

StubHub has thus displaced almost all the economic value once provided by scalpers and brokers. There's a new middleman in town, and it has made the market more competitive while lowering transaction costs for buyers and sellers. Vinny's Ticket Shop, the scalper in the parking lot, and Amy's website are under siege and may not survive. If they don't, what will replace them?

The Evolution of the Market III: The Future

Technology has already dramatically changed the economics of ticket resale. But it has not made much of an impact on how teams sell tickets in the first place. To be sure, there are some changes: Philips Arena, for instance, now goes directly to customers through Ticketmaster, when it once offered a first-sale contract to Amy. But as teams have been doing for decades, they are selling individual and season tickets to fans at the highest prices they can get.

Things are changing, however, as teams and leagues busily work on two initiatives—also borrowed from long-successful airline strategies—that they hope will noticeably increase ticket revenue. One of these ideas is good for the teams, and maybe for fans too. Economists are all for it. The other is an economic disaster waiting to happen.

First, the constructive venture: "dynamic pricing." This term is heard regularly from team ticket sales departments nowadays, but other industries have practiced the idea far longer. Hotels, for example, have known for years that it makes financial sense to vary prices based on factors like the day of the week, the time of year, and how many visitors are expected in town. Prices also change as the hotel gets an idea of how much availability remains on a given approaching day. In short, hotel rooms are a scarce resource, and when demand is high, hotel owners take advantage of this scarcity. More recently, Uber and other rideshare platforms have used dynamic pricing (known in this context as "surge pricing") to equate supply and demand based on current conditions.

Sports teams are only now starting to vary prices based on realized, up-to-the-minute demand. The first step teams took was to price different games based on expected willingness to pay. So the New York Yankees, for example, set much lower prices for a weekday game against the Oakland A's—my favorite team, but apparently not the country's—than for a Saturday night game against their archrival, the Boston Red Sox. This type of price discrimination, which follows the same logic as hotels charging more for days on which they expect less-price-sensitive business travelers, has slowly been creeping into the ticket market for years and is now fairly widespread.

Taking the same line of thinking a step further, dynamic pricing involves making a given game's tickets more and less expensive as demand ebbs and flows. Teams don't want to be perceived as unfair, and they especially don't want to alienate season ticket holders by making tickets available at low prices for those who wait, so they have been slow to adopt dynamic pricing. But teams in British soccer leagues and Major League Baseball have started to use dynamic pricing, and it has become a hot topic among sports executives.[9]

As the *Chicago Tribune* reported, "Want to go to the Cubs game against the Colorado Rockies this week? A check of the Cubs website Tuesday showed that a bleacher ticket for Monday night cost $19. On Wednesday, the same ticket cost $21. Why the $2 increase? Welcome to the world of dynamic pricing."[10] As with hotel room pricing, dynamic pricing models use a mix of computer algorithms and analyst decisions to generate a tailored ticket price based on the demand for any particular game.

Dynamic pricing will increase teams' ticket profits. One baseball executive says, "Dynamic pricing can lift average ticket prices 10 to 15 percent over the course of a season. During a playoff race, dynamic pricing can lift that percentage over the 20 percent average."[11] The economist Andrew Sweeting estimates the revenue increase at 16 percent. That is a valuable boost, but not a true game changer, given that ticket sales make up less than 30 percent of Major League Baseball revenues. The Arizona Diamondbacks, for example, reaped $54 million in ticket revenue in 2019, so a 15 percent bump in that number owing to dynamic pricing would yield an additional $8 million: good money, sure, but only about a quarter of the annual salary Arizona paid the pitcher Zack Greinke that year.[12]

Although the added revenue may not be dramatic, dynamic pricing allows teams to achieve another important goal: selling more tickets. Selling more seats matters to teams more than optimizing the price of individual tickets. Tickets can certainly be expensive, but they are often sold below the price the market would bear. Teams are willing to forgo some ticket revenue in the short term because having sellouts helps create interest in the team and, in turn, more ticket sales in the long term. Also, an empty seat is extremely costly to a team because of the loss of parking, concessions, and merchandise revenue.

It's probably not a surprise to hear that having high attendance numbers helps a team's reputation. As anyone who has seen an Ottawa Senators or Florida Panthers highlight on *SportsCenter* knows, it doesn't reflect well on those teams to have more people watching from the penalty box than from the stands.[13] Moreover, full stadiums heighten the overall fan experience, just as eating in a full restaurant can enhance one's enjoyment of the food.[14]

Teams want more people at their games because each additional fan brings a marginal increase in utility for the rest of the crowd. Additionally, benefits arise from large stadium audiences beyond the mere feeling that one is partaking in something popular. Many fans enjoy engaging in routines such as "the wave" or "Let's Go [Home

Team]" chants. Both of these rituals require a critical mass of fellow fans and increase many people's enjoyment of the game.

Furthermore, teams speculate in creating bigger fan bases in the future. Teams have a vested interest in inflating attendance today, even at the cost of a few dollars in short-term profit, because fans who have a good time at the game are more likely to return. Sports fandom can have a nearly addictive power; serious fans may feel compelled to check in on their favorite team even during dinner parties or weddings.[15]

In short, teams have strong incentives to get fans into the seats. And dynamic pricing may turn out to be a critical way for teams to keep their stadiums full without underpricing tickets as much as they might have needed to in the past. Moreover, dynamic pricing helps teams without hurting fans on the whole. True, a few people will pay more—those who used to line up to get Yankees–Red Sox tickets when they cost the same as Yankees-A's tickets—but teams are only helping fans allocate the tickets the way brokers helped allocate them in the old days. Dynamic pricing is here to stay, and most of us should be fine with it.

As for the second idea some teams are hoping to adopt from the airline industry—nontransferable tickets—I am not so optimistic.

You cannot sell your airline ticket to another passenger. Your name is on the ticket and boarding pass, and some combination of airport security and airline staff will stop you from getting on a plane with a ticket sold to someone else. Logistically, that kind of enforcement is tricky. Airlines can only stop you from using another person's ticket because they demand identification multiple times before you board.

Entry to games under this system would become more complicated than it is now, but there's no reason stadiums can't enact the same requirement: they could sell a ticket with your name on it and then ask for identification as you enter the stadium. Teams are reluctant to impose this burden on fans, however, both because it could slow stadium entry and because they don't want to alienate loyal season ticket holders, who would lose the ability to sell off or give away their tickets. Still, nontransferable tickets are becoming more common at concerts, where season ticket holders are not an issue.

Promoters generally appeal to the evil of scalpers to explain nontransferability. Resellers do impose extra costs on fans, either by requiring them to pay more than the listed price for tickets, or by making them spend time and resources to compete with brokers to buy tickets as soon as they become available. This problem has been exacerbated in recent years by the rise of bots—computer programs that buy tickets online as soon as they become available, strictly for the purpose of reselling those tickets at a profit later. Given how easy it is to write this kind of computer program, their proliferation has made the scalping market extremely competitive. Resellers lucky enough to get high-value tickets right away might make a nice margin on them, but for many others, the business is not very profitable.

A fan really has no reason to prefer to pay high prices directly to the teams rather than to brokers who manage to get tickets early and cheap, but somehow the creators of bots and other resellers continue to draw much more of the fans' wrath than team owners do. So teams are working to severely restrict resale, arguing that they are looking out for fans against those greedy ticket brokers.

More and more sports teams and leagues are making deals with a single resale channel to make them the "exclusive" ticket outlet. If you're interested in buying tickets to the NCAA Final Four men's or women's basketball tournament, for instance, you're likely to end up at PrimeSport.com. That's not because you will find their site more user-friendly than other options; odds are you've never heard of PrimeSport, and there's really nothing special about it relative to its competitors. You will end up at PrimeSport because the company has an exclusive arrangement with the NCAA. The NCAA does not sanction the selling of Final Four tickets on StubHub, and there is no guarantee of authenticity. StubHub cannot provide tickets to customers as seamlessly as PrimeSport.

Is that really a problem? Aren't tickets still available for resale? Well, yes. Because it has a quasi-monopoly, PrimeSport can charge a higher commission than it would if it had to compete on equal footing with StubHub. This added profit margin enables PrimeSport to pay the NCAA a handsome fee to be the exclusive agent, and the NCAA in turn increases its profits.

These types of arrangements are not as bad as pure monopolies, but they do stifle competition and hurt fans. Also, although teams claim to be looking out for fans' interests by cutting brokers out of the process, the teams are not trying to lower prices for fans but rather trying to capture the brokers' profits. The law professor Chris Sagers has glimpsed the future of ticket sales, and he warns that if laws are not passed to protect consumers, it may not be pretty. "Artists, promoters, teams and ticket companies," he argues, "want to restrict what fans can do with their tickets, and ultimately want to corner the now-lucrative resale market. They claim that their goal is to eliminate scalping, but the realities are that they will profit from ticket resale if they can control it, and they want to eliminate competition in resale markets in order to keep their initial ticket prices high. Sports teams are so committed to the latter goal that some secretly impose price floors on their affiliated resale exchanges, and some . . . have threatened to confiscate season tickets of fans who resell on competing exchanges."[16]

The "price floors" Sagers refers to are restrictions that prevent fans from selling tickets on an exclusive resale site for less than face value. Although these rules ostensibly protect season ticket holders' investments, in practice they lead to empty seats and many fans not going to a game that they would happily have attended if they could have bought a ticket at the market price. StubHub, the official resale site of Major League Baseball, allows people to sell tickets well below face value. This leads to more seats being sold but some unhappiness among sellers. Chris Tsakalakis, the former StubHub president, remembers being harassed at a cocktail party by an investment banker who owned San Francisco Giants season tickets. "He asked me, 'Can you do something so prices don't go below face value? I know how supply and demand work, but I don't like it for myself.'"

As teams and leagues impose more restrictions on resale and use dynamic pricing to fill seats without scalpers, what is the future of ticket scalping and brokering? I foresee two recent innovations turning into larger trends.

Amy's Tickets provides the first answer: value-added services that go beyond simple tickets. Economic forces are turning Amy's Tickets into Amy's VIP Events. Amy explained that Amy's VIP Events offers not only tickets but hospitality, hosting, and transportation. If you want to go to a major game or tournament and have it feel more like a wine mixer, you should call her. It's an upscale business for an expanding market—the American leisure class, with money to spend in search of a unique and memorable experience. This is Amy's future. "I am doing bigger events," she says, "and getting away from the day-in-and-day-out of selling tickets. The VIP side is definitely an area where I can grow."

The big ticket resellers are not far behind. StubHub throws a party for all its Super Bowl customers, for example, and PrimeSport hosts an array of "VIP Hospitality" offerings at the NCAA Men's Basketball Final Four, including sports bar games, drinks and food, and a chance to meet legends of college basketball. Amy's Tickets has a more personal touch, but it may be tough for her to stay ahead.

The other innovation with a promising future is yet another example of teams borrowing an idea from the airline industry: the up-grade. A few Major League Baseball teams have already rolled out an in-game upgrade program. If you get to the stadium and don't like your view—and you're not daring enough to try to sneak past the ushers guarding the better seats—you can now pull up a league-run app on your phone and pay to move to an empty seat in a better location. Every game has a few no-shows or some people who never succeeded in reselling their extra tickets. Through in-game resale apps, the "invisible hand" of the market can better use those resources while also earning teams a little profit.

Upgrades can also help make the stadium look and feel more full, enhancing the game experience. Teams that have a no-show prob-lem, like the Yankees, are especially likely to employ this scheme. The Yankees charge an arm and a leg for good seats because New York is full of rich financiers who give the seats to clients, entertain at the stadium, and even occasionally take their families to a Yankees game. There's only one problem: these ticket holders often don't bother showing up. The journalist Chris Connors lamented "the glaring number of empty seats in the lower levels of the stadium" and noted that "the Yankees continue to undermine many of their most dedi-cated fans by pricing them out of the most coveted seats in their palatial residence."[17] The no-show "fans" with great seats alienate the poorer but more avid fans sitting in the upper decks.

If the no-show seats can be filled with those more devoted fans through upgrades, the atmosphere at Yankee Stadium will improve, and the Yankees can siphon a bit more money from their loyal fol-lowers. There is, however, an impediment that may keep upgrades from becoming the norm. The journalist Tom Ley concludes that the Yankees do not "want the kind of riff-raff that buys cheap tickets on StubHub mixing with rich fans who pay full price to sit in the same section."[18] For now, upgrades are making inroads with teams that have fewer super-rich fans, like my local favorite Oakland A's.[19]

Perhaps some team will think outside the box and try a promising solution to the empty-seats problem: give tickets away. Could a team do better by just giving tickets away on a first-come-first-serve basis and making up the lost ticket revenue from concession sales and the goodwill of its fans, which would presumably pay off in higher viewership and more expensive TV rights? Although I would love to see a team experiment with free tickets, it is hard to see it becoming the hot new trend. Ticket sales are small compared with TV rights, but they do bring in a big chunk of revenue that concessions would not replace. Also, if people didn't pay for their tickets, they might not feel as invested in the game and might even skip it if they got busy or the weather was not perfect. Perhaps, in this scenario, no-shows would make the stadium emptier than when prices are high. But, most important, free tickets would probably not end up being free; bots and brokers would gobble up the good seats and then resell them. Owners have learned to tolerate letting brokers have some of the profit from ticket sales—but don't count on their giving *all* the profit to brokers.

The past and the present have been good to ticket holders: the thicker market has made it easier to buy and sell. We can hope the future looks even brighter, but as teams get more sophisticated, be ready for them to continue to figure out ways to squeeze more money from ticket sales and to cut out the scalpers. Perhaps governments around the world will protect buyers and resale markets, but given the teams' long history of shaping public opinion against scalpers, I wouldn't count on it.

8

Why Should You Be Upset If Your Hometown Hosts the Olympics?

Nursultan Nazarbayev has always been good at getting what he wants. Born to nomadic parents, he rose through the political apparatus in his native Kazakhstan, and in 1989—when Kazakhstan was still part of the Soviet Union—he became the leader of the state. Four years later, he became the first president of independent Kazakhstan, a position he retained for thirty years by regularly getting reelected with over 90 percent of the vote. He was, of course, functionally a dictator, though opinions vary on whether he was a benevolent one. Under his control, the resource-rich country did reasonably well economically and formed close ties with Russia.[1]

Yet Nazarbayev could not attain one thing he seemed to truly crave: international recognition for himself and his country. Kazakhstan is best known, at least in the United States, as the home of Sacha Baron Cohen's fictional character Borat. Although Kazakhstan is larger in area than western Europe, it's likely that few western Europeans could pick it out on a map. Even fewer have heard of Nazarbayev. His attempts to bring renown to his country, which include paying the former British prime minister Tony Blair millions of dollars for advice and exchanging public praise with former Italian prime minister Silvio Berlusconi, don't seem to have helped much.

Consequently, Nazarbayev tried another tack: Almaty, Kazakhstan's biggest city, put together a bid for hosting the Winter Olympics in 2022. The effort was initially dismissed as a long shot; observers noted the country's relative anonymity, remote location, and sketchy human rights record.[2] But the bid began to attract attention. Kazakhstan hoped to use the Olympics to "make a big splash on the world stage," the *New York Times* reported. "It is a springboard for conquering new heights," Nazarbayev crowed to the press. "Kazakhstan should be known as a nation of winners."

In the end, though, Nazarbayev's big moment was snatched away. In the summer of 2015, the Olympic Committee announced that the Games were being awarded to Beijing. The decision gave some indication of the committee's low esteem for Kazakhstan, given that Beijing's drawbacks include terrible air pollution, getting so little snow in its nearby mountains that it needs tons of environmentally concerning manmade snow, a plan to spread the events over hundreds of miles, and having recently hosted the Summer Olympics.

How and why did the choice for 2022 come down to two flawed cities in countries ruled by repressive regimes? As it turns out, the warped economic incentives behind hosting big sporting events almost gave Nazarbayev his big shot. Only maligned or ignored nations, anxious to display their greatness, were willing to waste the money and effort.

This international lack of interest in hosting is a new phenomenon; in 2013, when the Olympic Committee first requested bids for the 2022 games, many cities seriously began the process of bidding, and six cities ultimately prepared detailed proposals. Soon, however, the trouble began. First Stockholm backed out because of political opposition in Sweden. In May 2014, Krakow, Poland, held a referendum on its bid and, after finding its citizenry opposed, withdrew as well. Lviv, Ukraine, withdrew shortly afterward in light of a domestic political crisis. That withdrawal left Oslo as the leading contender:

Norway had once hosted a successful Olympics, was swimming in money thanks to high oil prices at the time, and is a perennial leader in the Winter Olympic medal count. But in October 2014, after being named a finalist along with Almaty and Beijing, Oslo also dropped out owing to overwhelming local opposition.[3]

What the residents of Oslo, Stockholm, and Krakow recognized is that hosting the Olympics means three weeks of revelry followed by years of economic fallout. Massive public investments that could be directed toward needed government programs are instead used for constructing large stadiums and other athletic facilities. The economist Alan Blinder once said that "economists have the least influence on policy where they know the most and are most agreed."[4] He had in mind practices like rent control and trade barriers, both of which are derided by virtually every economist, yet still persist. But as the economists John Siegfried and Andrew Zimbalist have written, "Few fields of empirical economic research offer virtual unanimity of findings. Yet, independent work on the economic impact of stadiums and arenas has uniformly found that there is no statistically significant positive correlation between sports facility construction and economic development."[5] Economists' skepticism regarding Olympic and World Cup bids is decades old. Only recently, however, as the dearth of bids for the 2022 Games shows, have politicians and taxpayers shown signs of waning enthusiasm for these investments.

The problem comes down to two pervasive economic phenomena: "agency problems" (that is, misalignment of interests between the people who make a decision and those who pay for it) and old-fashioned corruption. Consider three examples:

- Vladimir Putin essentially decided, on behalf of all of Russia, to spend without limit on the 2014 Winter Games in Sochi. The final price tag of $51 billion made the 2014 Games the most expensive Olympics ever, summer or winter. In preparation for the Games, for example, Russia built a rail link from the Olympic Village to the ski events. It extended thirty-one miles and cost $8.7 billion, three times the amount that NASA spent on the newest generation of Mars rovers. The head of the railway agency that built the link is a close associate of Putin's and has ties to local banks and to the two companies that were given the contract without competitive bidding.[6]

- The state of Wisconsin agreed, in 2015, to pay $250 million toward building an arena for the NBA's Milwaukee Bucks. After accounting for interest and many hidden costs, the true price to taxpayers will be much greater. The team is owned by the hedge fund managers Wes Edens and Marc Lasry, each of whom is worth a couple of billion dollars, but they nonetheless threatened to move the Bucks if the arena was not publicly funded. The state's commitment to the arena was approved by Governor Scott Walker in the same year that he signed legislation authorizing $300 million in budget cuts for Wisconsin's public universities.[7]

- Perhaps the only sports event that can compare with the Olympics in terms of wasted public resources is the World Cup. Qatar won the rights to host the World Cup in 2022 through outright bribery of the officials responsible for deciding where the event would be held. The cheating was necessary because there is literally no other reason to hold the World Cup in Qatar: it has sweltering temperatures, very few appropriate athletic venues, and no noteworthy soccer tradition. It has never previously qualified for the World Cup, though by virtue of hosting will do so in 2022. The event had to be scheduled for the late fall to avoid the worst of the summer heat. Qatar naturalized a number of talented African players to try (unsuccessfully, it turned out) to put together a team that could qualify for the 2018 World Cup, and the government has set about building a collection of new stadiums at fabulous expense.[8] Zimbalist estimates that Qatar will lose approximately $200 billion on the event.[9]

The common thread in each of these and countless other examples is that individuals had the power to decide how a much larger group of people spent their money. This misalignment of interests led to an elected or self-declared leader making financial decisions that hurt constituents while making himself or herself better off.

Still, hopeful news is on the horizon. Fans and citizens are pushing back against the idea of taxpayers shelling out for sports events and facilities. Will they save cities from frittering away money? Maybe, although those who champion Olympic bids are trying to stay a step ahead of those who insist on fiscal responsibility.

A Walk in the (Olympic) Park

The people who lead Olympic bids, as well as those who advocate building new stadiums, argue that the events create lasting economic vitality. But these claims simply hold no water. To get a sense of the problems with the hosting logic, consider what is widely accepted as one of the more financially successful Olympic Games: the London Summer Olympics in 2012.[10]

The newly built venues in the area the London organizers called "Olympic Park" include the Aquatics Center, at a cost of $460 million; the Basketball Arena, $62 million; the Velodrome, for cycling, $180 million; the Riverbank Arena, for field hockey, $32 million; the Water Polo Arena, $46 million; the Copper Box, for team handball *preliminary* matches, $75 million; and, of course, the Olympic Stadium, for track and field, which cost $832 million. For those keeping score at home, that's a grand total of *$1.69 billion*—and that money did not cover hosting sports like fencing, surfing, or beach volleyball, all of which required upgrades to existing facilities.[11]

What has happened to those facilities since the Olympics? The Aquatics Center, after significant and costly post-Olympics renovations, opened to the public in 2014. The Basketball Arena, which was designed to be portable, was dismantled and put up for sale, but it has never been reported as sold. The Riverbank Arena and Water Polo Arena were demolished shortly after the conclusion of the Games. The Velodrome remains in place as a potentially top-flight indoor cycling venue, but the British national team decided to keep its training base in Manchester. The Copper Box has hosted events such as home games for club basketball and handball teams and a mixed martial arts showcase. The Olympic Stadium was given *for free* to the soccer team West Ham United F.C. and subsequently converted into a full-time soccer stadium for an additional $400 million, most of which was covered by the British government. It's worth noting that even before the Olympics, London already had several large stadiums, each of which was used about twenty times per year.

The revenues from those two and a half weeks of the Olympics needed to be otherworldly to compensate for the costs of hosting them. The Games brought some added attention to London and may well have brought some added tourism and new business deals. But it is hard to make the case that the city of London would not have been better off spending $14 billion on something else (like improving transportation or retraining workers who have lost manufacturing jobs, both of which have longer-lasting benefits), rather than hosting a glorified showcase of archery and fencing. And remember: the London version has been generally accepted as a relatively successful Olympics, financially; such events often waste even more money.

The Faulty Logic in Favor of Public Financing

Team owners, much like politicians justifying an Olympic bid, also push cities to build stadiums with promises of financial windfalls. A team wanting its home city to build a new facility for it obviously does not take the position that the venue's construction is likely to incur massive losses. Instead it rolls out a series of reports by economists and developers—all, of course, on the team payroll—showing why the new structure is guaranteed to bring an economic boom. Given that it's not hard to brainstorm ways in which a sparkling new arena or ballpark might help a city's economy, we can charitably suppose that the people who write these reports believe their claims hold at least some water.

Consider Golden 1 Center, the arena built for the Sacramento Kings in 2016. The city of Sacramento, which is on the hook for $255 million of the estimated $477 million construction cost, created a website to promote the deal to its taxpayers. One of the FAQs concerned the new arena's financial benefits; the city's answer was that the project would "increase the vitality of downtown areas" through the specific avenues of "investment from businesses," "sales, property, hotel, and utility tax revenues," and "thousands of jobs during construction . . . and hundreds of permanent positions."

The Kings' idea was that businesses would want to move to the same neighborhood as the hot new arena because it would attract fans, who would then frequent the new businesses on their way to or from a game, thus growing the local economy. Add in the resulting tax gains for the government and the extra jobs created for residents, and this proposition sounds pretty promising.

But do these benefits actually accrue to the area around the sports venue? In the case of Golden 1 Center, things have gone much better than you might expect. First of all, the final cost was about $560 million, just 17 percent over budget. Also, because Sacramento's city government did an unusually good job of negotiating the contract, the Kings' owners paid for all of the $83 million cost overrun. That, sadly, is a huge victory by the standards of American professional sports stadiums.

As to the arena's benefits, the Downtown Sacramento Partnership issued a fact sheet listing Golden 1 Center's accomplishments on its second anniversary. The document notes tremendous property sales and investments, as well as large increases in employment, in downtown Sacramento in the first two years of the arena's life. It also notes that downtown office vacancy rates are at a five-year low and that downtown foot traffic is up substantially.

Those facts are all true, and it certainly seems that the new arena did not hurt the local economy. But did it help? Answering this question requires knowing two things: what would have happened if the city had not built the arena, and how did the economic activity in the area around the arena affect the economic activity of nearby areas?

From 2015 to 2018 (the time of Golden 1 Center's construction and its first two years of use), several trends that had nothing to do with the arena affected the Sacramento business environment. The economy was booming, with the city's unemployment rate dropping from 6.0 percent to 3.9 percent; demographics favored downtown markets such as the area around Golden 1 Center; people were fleeing the increasingly expensive Bay Area to smaller cities like Sacramento; property values boomed; and office vacancy rates dropped in all major cities anywhere near Sacramento. (To illustrate that the phenomenon of local property value growth was not confined to Sacramento, note that the vacancy rate in Reno, a somewhat smaller city 130 miles to the east, fell at the same rate as Sacramento's, while the second tech bubble in San Francisco, ninety miles to the west, made Sacramento's vibrant center look like a one-horse town.) In short, Sacramento boomed at the same time that the Golden 1 Center was being built and opened, but it would have gone through a strong period of economic development in any case.

The Downtown Sacramento Partnership had lots of good numbers to back up its argument. But the right way to evaluate the city's $255 million public investment isn't to look at how the area did; it's to ask if that $255 million was used effectively. The true economic cost of the arena includes both the direct cost and the *opportunity cost.* Any given purchase is worthwhile only if its benefits outweigh its cost *and* if it is the most efficient use of the resources used to make it. Imagine entering a thrift shop in which everything costs exactly $1 with a single dollar bill in your pocket. Suppose you find a valuable baseball card worth $25 and an old Super Bowl ticket worth $20. If you only had a dollar to spend, you would obviously make a profit buying the ticket, but you would forgo an even greater profit by not buying the card. Buying the ticket is thus a poor allocation of your very scarce resources—your one dollar.

The same applies to stadium deals. Sacramento's $255 million commitment to the Kings is modest on the grand scale of publicly financed arenas, and its population is on the smaller end of major-league sports cities. To the city's credit, Sacramento made sure it would not pay for cost overruns and seems to have done other things to encourage economic development in the area. Just as London was an example of an Olympics that minimized the damage, Golden 1 Center did not bleed ungodly amounts of public money.

Still, rather than build a new arena for a wealthy NBA team, the city could have used that $255 million to employ more than two hundred public workers for $50,000 a year for twenty-five years. It could have built better roads or better water systems to manage the area's frequent droughts; it could have funded a 1,000 percent increase in the endowment of Sacramento State University, which already generates over $800 million for the local economy every year; or it could have made a large dent in the city's $2 billion pension plan deficit. Sacramento didn't really have $255 million to spend, but since it decided to do so, any of these investments would almost certainly have returned more to the city's economy than the $255 million contribution to the new arena. And yet the city government pushed the deal, and Golden 1 Center now hosts lots of Kings' games and other events every year.

Sacramento made a mistake. Study after study by economists shows that for the investment involved, stadiums and arenas never produce a favorable return on taxpayer dollars. Even when the area around a facility does well, it only draws economic activity that would have gone to other forms of entertainment a few miles away. As Siegfried and Zimbalist put it, "While sports teams may rearrange the spending and economic activity in an urban area, they are not likely to add much to it."

Why don't stadiums and arenas provide a return on taxpayer dollars? We can identify several possible reasons, all of which probably contribute.

First, the stadium almost always costs more than initially estimated, and the government is usually expected to come up with the extra money. Those pushing the deal have an incentive to underestimate the cost to get it approved, and for some reason, city after city falls for this trick. As a result, the city is implicitly in debt even before the venue opens its doors. But this phenomenon may be slowly going out of style. As noted, Sacramento drew the line here and ensured that the team covered the cost overruns. Likewise, when voters in the city of Arlington, Texas, approved $500 million of public funding for a baseball stadium for the Texas Rangers, they did so on the condition that the Rangers would be responsible for all cost increases. If cities continue to fund sports venues, let's hope they will at least follow Sacramento and Arlington and not write a blank check.[12]

Second, the jobs that a team supposedly adds to the community are minimum-wage and part-time jobs. A basketball team like the Kings plays forty-one home games a year, not counting playoff games, for perhaps three hours a night. Even adding concerts and other events at the venue, a concessions or parking lot employee will only get a few hundred work hours per year—not exactly the kind of job that's likely to keep someone gainfully employed for long periods of time. And those job gains are likely offset by fewer people needed (or lower tip earnings) at entertainment venues a few miles away that are less crowded each night the arena is in use.

Third, the supposed ripple effect in the surrounding community caused by the stadium's presence simply doesn't exist. Businesses within a block or two of the stadium inarguably see a sales boost from incoming and outgoing fans. But no study has ever shown that a new stadium pumps additional money into the city as a whole, and several have shown conclusively that it does not.[13]

Finally, cities have no negotiating power because they are on the wrong side of a supply-and-demand imbalance. There is only one Olympic Committee; there are only two Olympic Games every four years. Similarly, there are only about thirty teams in each major sports league. In the game of musical chairs, mega-events and teams are the chairs, while the cities are the kids rushing not to get left out.

For a team, the threat of moving to a more welcoming city is a valuable trump card. A natural consequence of the relative scarcity of teams is that several large cities don't have one. Four top-20 metropolitan areas (San Diego, Seattle, Saint Louis, and Baltimore) lack a basketball team, and five top-30 metropolitan areas (Charlotte, Portland, San Antonio, Orlando, and Sacramento) lack a baseball team. Meanwhile, only twelve metropolitan areas host teams in all four major sports, meaning that many of the country's largest cities are a constant threat to poach a team from an underperforming smaller city.

Because so many cities want a team, relocation becomes an easy bargaining chip anytime an existing team wants a new stadium. The Kings, for instance, had all but packed their bags for Seattle before a new Sacramento ownership coalition came together to promise a state-of-the-art new venue. Several well-known relocations have been driven by a hunt for stadium deals. Back in the 1950s, the desire for a new stadium—more accurately, a difference of opinion over where to build it—was at least part of the reason that the Dodgers moved from Brooklyn to Los Angeles. In 1997, the lure of new facilities led the Houston Oilers to become the Tennessee Titans and the Hartford Whalers to become the Carolina Hurricanes.[14] Few teams actually move for a new facility, however, because the incumbent city usually ponies up when a team threatens to leave.

If a city is being realistic, building an arena can never be justified on solely financial grounds. Economists Roger Noll and Andrew Zimbalist once suggested that everybody would be better off if the government took a fraction of the money it might spend on a stadium and just gave it directly to the team as a bribe to not leave town.[15] But does another valid reason exist to back a stadium, an Olympic bid, or a World Cup? After all, the games are a lot of fun.

Can You Really Put a Price on a Day at the Park?

Although publicly funded sports facilities invariably prove to be awful investments, an economist can still rationalize the cost if a stadium provides the public with enough nonfinancial benefits. Happiness, or utility, carries legitimate economic value that you can't always put a price on. If you buy a $1,500 ticket to sit in the front row above the Yankees dugout for a playoff game, it's not because you expect to catch a foul ball and toss it to Aaron Judge for a $2,000 autograph. It's because the enjoyment and memories you'll get from attending the game are worth $1,500 to you. Similarly, maybe cities know full well that they aren't going to recoup the cost of a $500 million stadium, but they think that the happiness their citizens derive from having the team in town is worth $500 million.

If this were true, it would provide an elegant solution to the riddle of publicly financed stadium deals; maybe citizens know that the financial contribution of stadiums and events is a fiction, but they feel the nonfinancial benefits outweigh the costs.

Maybe, but probably not. A group of economists did a study of the 2012 London Games using surveys that measured the happiness of people in London (relative to other cities) around the time of the Olympics. The economists found that people in London did feel happier during the beginning and end of the Olympics. But their calculations suggested that the happiness the Games created, if translated into dollars using economic techniques for determining people's willingness to pay to be made happier, was not enough to make up for the cost of the Games unless the benefits extended to much of the United Kingdom. They also found that the happiness people felt was limited to the time of the Games themselves and did not last through a follow-up survey a year later.[16]

Another reason to think the warm glow of stadiums and Olympics does not outweigh the financial costs is the growing public expression of disapproval. As mentioned earlier, negative public opinion led Oslo and other cities to withdraw their bids for the 2022 Winter Olympics. Recent polls and an accumulating pile of "no" outcomes on voter referenda further suggest opposition to public expenditures on sports investments. A nationwide poll of Americans in 2014 showed that 69 percent opposed public financing of NFL stadiums. This trend has been reflected in recent votes. The last three new venues for MLB, NBA, NFL, or NHL teams to receive voter approval for public financing were all in the sports-crazy Dallas metropolitan area: the aforementioned Arlington stadium vote in 2016, the Cowboys' stadium in Arlington in 2004, and the NHL Dallas Stars arena in 1998.[17] Outside of Texas, voters simply do not want to spend their tax dollars on expensive new venues for professional sports teams.

In truth, however, public approval is not necessary for arena-hungry investors. Case in point: the Charlotte Hornets' arena deal was rejected by 57 to 43 percent in a public referendum, but city council members nevertheless pushed through a different plan, estimated to cost the public more than $250 million.

A classic example of well-connected people going behind the backs of taxpayers to build a publicly financed stadium is SunTrust Park, home of the Atlanta Braves baseball team since 2017. John Schuerholz, president of the Braves, said that the plan succeeded only because "it didn't leak out. If this deal had leaked out, it would not have gotten done." He made this statement after the public announcement of the deal prompted groups as diverse as the Atlanta Tea Party and the local chapter of the Sierra Club to hold an unsuccessful joint demonstration against it.[18]

Another noneconomic idea that might contribute to politicians pushing for sports facilities and events is unrealistic optimism. Did the Braves' management team and the Cobb County commissioners (or, for that matter, the people behind the London Olympic bid, the Sacramento arena, and other previous publicly funded sports investments) know they were trying to pull the wool over citizens' eyes? Or had they talked themselves into believing that they were doing the best thing for their communities and that they had to keep it quiet to avoid letting shortsighted activists defeat a great idea? Nobody will ever know, but it also doesn't matter; either way, selfishness and self-deception are equally wasteful.

Fat-Cat Local Politicians

The idea that citizens might derive enough joy from a stadium or event to justify it seems unlikely at best. Why, then, do cities keep bidding for the Olympics and offering to build mind-numbingly expensive new sports venues? One simple answer is that, like most other public policy decisions, the choice of whether or not to fund the stadium isn't made by citizens. It's made by politicians.

The disparity between politicians' and voters' attitudes toward stadium deals underscores a larger economic issue known as "agency problems." An agency problem arises when a person or group of people is given the power to decide how to use resources that are not their own, and whose use affects some other group's well-being. A good example is a CEO and the board of directors whose primary responsibility is to increase their company's value for shareholders. Despite that mandate, CEOs engage in pet projects and negotiate lavish pay packages all the time. Just as CEOs get board members to go along with their schemes at shareholder expense, team owners get politicians to pony up the taxpayers' money.

Representative democracies create agency problems at every level. Spending taxpayers' money is, of course, necessary: society would struggle to form fire departments, distribute welfare, or preserve public land if elected officials did not govern the administration of those processes. But it is impossible to perfectly align officeholders' incentives with those of their constituents.

Although voters almost never think that using tax money to fund a team's new digs is a good idea, their elected representatives often feel differently. If a politician thinks he will personally derive enough utility from constructing the new stadium to make up for whatever small minority of voters will base their voting decision on their dislike for the stadium deal, he will do it.

The personal utility of a new stadium to a politician could come from a couple of different sources. For example, voters who did not approve of increasing the hospital tax may nonetheless like their mayor better after seeing him break ground for their favorite team's fancy new arena. Perhaps rabid fans base their voting decisions on these sorts of events, whereas most voters, though they don't want a new stadium, don't care enough to let such issues be a driving factor in their voting. Or perhaps the politician is a fan of the team. Imagine you were elected mayor of the city in which you grew up, and your favorite team started griping about its antiquated facility and wondering in public whether Las Vegas might be willing to build the team a fancier one. Might you round up a few hundred million of your constituents' tax dollars and offer to build one right there in town?

Taxpayers in Hamilton County, Ohio, home to the city of Cincinnati, were whipped by one particularly cruel display of agency problems. In 1995, the NFL's Cincinnati Bengals started making it known that if they did not get a new, publicly funded stadium, they would buy a one-way ticket to Baltimore. At the same time, baseball's Cincinnati Reds also decided to demand a new home. For reasons related to "downtown development" and other familiar catchphrases, local politicians began to negotiate with both teams.

Representatives from the Reds and Bengals, the city of Cincinnati, and Hamilton County eventually reached a deal to finance the two stadiums for a combined cost of $500 million by increasing the county sales tax by 0.5 percent. So far, not too bad: the tax increase was small, the teams agreed to stay in town, and a lot of people came away happy. Very quickly, however, it became clear that neither stadium was going to come in at its expected cost. The completed Bengals field eventually cost nearly $500 million by itself, and with the Reds' field over budget as well, the final price tag for the two venues was $792 million. Here's how the *New York Times* described the terms of the county's deal with the Bengals:

> The team had to pay rent only through 2009 on its 26-year lease, and has to cover the cost of running the stadium only for game days. Starting in 2017, the county will reimburse the team for these costs, too. The county will pay $8.5 million this year to keep the stadium going. The Bengals keep revenue from naming rights, advertising, tickets, suites and most parking. If the county wants to recoup money by taxing tickets, concessions or parking, it needs the team's approval.[19]

Now that the deal has tanked so badly, you might imagine that the people responsible for it are long gone from local government. And they are, in a way; Hamilton county commissioner Bob Bedinghaus, the most enthusiastic member of the county board that approved the deal, was voted out of office in 2000. But he didn't spend much time looking for a job: shortly after his failed reelection campaign, he was hired as director of business development by none other than the Bengals. He worked in the team's front office for eighteen years.

Corruption

When the stakes are high enough, the misalignment between decision makers with big power and the constituents they represent can make the leap from "agency problems" to outright corruption.[20] Many in the United States like to think that corruption is something that happens in developing countries, Russia, and maybe in the negotiation of a few New Jersey sanitation contracts. But even Salt Lake City, with its squeaky-clean reputation, is not immune.

In 1991 the city finished just four votes behind Nagano, Japan, in its bid for the 1998 Winter Olympics. Officials supporting the Salt Lake bid were convinced that the loss was a consequence of their failure to court the representatives of developing countries, an emerging voting bloc under the International Olympic Committee's globalization efforts. Determined to land the 2002 Games, the Salt Lake City bid's backers lavished African and Latin American IOC officials with all-expenses-paid trips to Utah, tuition help and internships in the United States for their children, and campaign donations. When the committee convened in 1995 to select a host, Salt Lake won a decisive fifty-four-vote majority over the other four candidates on the first ballot.

The scandal that ensued as details emerged of Salt Lake's voter courtship efforts underscored a predictable problem with many bidding processes: the ultimate decision was made by a group of people who didn't have much interest in the outcome. In the case of the Olympics, host cities are elected by the general body of the IOC, which is composed of one hundred or more members from a wide range of countries around the world.

In theory, the IOC's members should all share an interest in maximizing the quality of the Olympics as a whole, but in practice, many of them are probably more concerned with their country's or their own welfare. After all, why would a representative from Samoa or Sudan care about whether the Winter Olympics are held in Utah or Sweden? No one from his country is going to participate, and it's unlikely that either site will do a vastly better job of hosting than the other.

The main thing people on the Salt Lake bid committee were guilty of—besides maybe a federal crime or two—was participating in a system of broken incentives. Only two ways exist to win an Olympic bid: either you can put together a great, detailed proposal that makes it clear your city is the best choice for a host, or you can scratch the backs of the people who make the decision. The former approach is more noble, but it's really just a crapshoot if you don't do some of the latter as well. If you think there was a big difference between Salt Lake City's winning bid and the bids of its top rivals Östersund, Sweden, and Sion, Switzerland, think again. Both cities put together strong bids, and then politics and luck sorted the rest out.

After the Salt Lake scandal, the International Olympic Committee changed the rules to try to discourage corruption. For example, site selectors may no longer fly to potential locations to be courted by an aspiring city. One theory about why Beijing was given the 2022 Winter Games instead of Almaty, Kazakhstan, is that IOC voters could not travel to Kazakhstan and therefore had only uninformed and vague images of the country. This theory suggests that the change in IOC rules may lessen the opportunities for corruption, but at the cost of leading to overly conservative host city selections.

On the other hand, it would not be unreasonable to worry, based on Nursultan Nazarbayev's reputation, about the persuasive techniques he might have used had the committee visited. If the IOC had not changed its rules, perhaps some Kazakh oil money would have found its way into the bank accounts of IOC officials and selectors. In any case, Nazarbayev did not get his Olympics, which means you will have to get used to artificial snow if you go to the Beijing Games in 2022, and you will have to find some other reason to visit Kazakhstan.

Getting cities to bid for the Olympics or to build a stadium continues to get harder as voters have woken up to the costs. Voters continue to stifle attempts to build large new stadiums. For the 2026 Winter Olympics, despite much early interest, voters in Calgary (Canada), Graz (Austria), and Sion (Switzerland) all squashed bids led by local politicians looking to make a name for themselves, and other cities also withdrew under public pressure. The Covid-19 pandemic will surely make overcoming citizens' objections even more difficult, given the massive losses Tokyo faced when forced to delay the 2020 Olympics by a year and to hold the Games with no international spectators, and the huge losses of money to cities as stadiums sat idle for more than a year during the pandemic (leading Sacramento to dip into its rainy-day fund to pay off bonds on the Golden 1 Center). Meanwhile, Nursultan Nazarbayev is enjoying the quiet life of retirement, and his country's citizens are lucky he didn't leave behind a large Olympic bill.

9

Who Wins When People Gamble?

The Cleveland Browns, long one of the doormats of the National Football League, got off to an encouraging start in the 2020 season, having won four of their first six games. But things were not looking good for the Browns in their seventh game when, with a little over a minute left to play, the promising Cincinnati Bengals rookie Joe Burrow threw a touchdown pass to give his team a 37–34 lead. Yet the Browns' upstart quarterback Baker Mayfield used that final minute to complete four straight passes and drive the Browns seventy-five yards, culminating with Mayfield's fifth touchdown pass of the day. With eleven seconds to go, the Browns led by three points, and the victory was almost iced. Cody Parkey, the Browns' placekicker, came on and missed the extra point. The missed kick had no bearing on the game. The Browns won, and Cleveland fans celebrated.

But some people, far from Paul Brown Stadium in Cincinnati, ignored the Browns' victory and instead focused on Parkey's seemingly meaningless missed kick. The Browns had been favored to win by three and a half points, and the missed extra point attempt prevented them from covering the spread. Some of the most vocal reactions to the Browns' win on Twitter came from people who had bet on the Browns and lost because of Parkey's miss. One gambler tweeted, "Cody Parkey . . . thanks man, that missed extra point only cost me a couple thousand. No problem."[1] Of course, lots of people who had bet on the Bengals were very happy (though few of them took the trouble to thank Parkey for their winnings).

If Parkey upset many bettors, he was a godsend to Las Vegas sportsbooks, for whom that day in October was overall the worst of the season. Gamblers tend to pick favorites at higher rates than underdogs, and as a result, a disproportionate share of money was bet on the Browns, whose failure to cover the spread meant a loss for gamblers as a whole but a win for Las Vegas sportsbooks. The sportsbooks don't care much about any given game: they expect to lose money on some games every Sunday but win on enough others to make money anyway.

This particular Sunday, however, was different. Popular favorites Tampa Bay (with their self-proclaimed "golden boy" quarterback Tom Brady), defending Super Bowl champion Kansas City, and the Los Angeles Chargers all won that day. Gamblers who submitted a sheet filled with nothing but the day's strongest favorites won big; those who did so as part of a parlay—a gambling strategy in which each bet's winnings are levied into a bigger bet for the next game—made a fortune. According to one bookie, "We lost four of our top five decisions. That pretty much decided the day for us." He reported a six-figure loss for his casino. In one day, businesses took big losses, while a few lucky guys sitting on couches or in bars had the most lucrative day of their lives by doing very nearly nothing.[2]

If you think about it, it's odd that one split-second bad decision or one amazing stroke of luck by a man on a football field or basketball court can deeply affect the finances of a completely unrelated person thousands of miles away. But that's the nature of sports gambling. The only somewhat comparable industry is the stock market. But at least the stock market arguably performs a valuable economic function by helping to finance commerce, and in any case, few people who don't work in finance spend hours each week watching stocks move up and down. Sports gamblers, however, do exactly that—and if they can't do it in Nevada or the growing list of municipalities where gambling on sports is legal, they do it illegally online. All of this gambling is driven by economic forces, has a major economic impact, raises ethical issues, and allows some well-informed groups to take advantage of (or, if you look at it more optimistically, entertain and excite) naive thrill seekers. There's a lot at stake. So should people be allowed to gamble legally on sports? The answer is a clear yes. Or no. But one thing is for sure: you should only gamble if you can afford to lose, because the odds are stacked against you.

Why Do People Gamble?

Just about every casual gambler falls into one of two categories: rational gamblers, whose inevitable losses are compensated for by the thrill of betting; and problem gamblers, whose ever escalating losses pile up as they feed an unhealthy addiction. The big difference between the two is the level of regret: rational gamblers lament their losses but accept that they are part of the overall experience, while irrational gamblers are inevitably surprised that they have lost and regret the choices their earlier selves have imposed on their later selves.

How can gambling be rational? The simple answer is "utility." If someone has a lot more fun watching a game after putting ten dollars down on one of the teams, the bet might be worth it even if he loses. Many people would pay ten dollars to enjoy a movie, so why shouldn't those people spend ten dollars to increase their enjoyment of a basketball game they otherwise wouldn't care about?

Rational-pleasure gambling accounts for the bulk of money that flows to bookies during the Super Bowl. The Super Bowl is an event that most Americans feel almost compelled to watch, but it can be hard to care about the actual game. Relatively few Americans feel strongly about, for instance, the San Francisco 49ers or the Kansas City Chiefs, the contestants in Super Bowl LIV.[3] A random fan in Oklahoma, watching at home with friends and family, might have a lot more fun if he bets a couple of bucks on the 49ers or on either team scoring a touchdown in the first five minutes of the third quarter. For that fan and millions of others who make similar bets, that couple of bucks generates enough added fun, win or lose, to be worth the wager. This phenomenon leads to the large array of available Super Bowl prop bets, ranging from which team will win the coin flip to the color of Gatorade poured on the winning coach.

Casual bets between friends can be fun and on balance don't cost people anything. One friend wins and the other loses. But as soon as a bookie gets involved, be it a guy at the office or a casino with a legal sportsbook, the expected return becomes negative. The primary reason is that on every bet, the bookie keeps a "vig" and gives you less than a full return if you win. If you pick the Green Bay Packers to beat the spread on a given Sunday, for example, you have to accept that you lose $11 when the bet fails but win only $10 when the Packers cover. Bookies stay in business by charging a fee. If a bookie has equal numbers of bets on both sides of a game, the bookie reaps 10 percent of the amount won by people who win the bet.

That 10 percent fee is money well spent if it makes the average fan a little bit happier, and in many situations, betting works that way. Wagers on landmark events like the Super Bowl and NCAA Basketball Tournament are social opportunities that enhance the experience of watching the event. In addition, lots of people enjoy investing in teams or people they support. Taking this pursuit to an extreme, the golfer Rory McIlroy's father famously scored £100,000 after his £200 bet on his son to win the British Open within ten years, placed when Rory was fifteen, came out a winner.[4] McIlroy's father may have believed he had inside information about his son's abilities that actually made his bet rational, but he just as likely thought that betting on the family's fairy-tale scenario would be a fun, slightly wasteful, but certainly affordable way to spend a few hundred pounds.

The Bookies Bet, Too

In some betting markets, the fee is all the bookmaker takes in—though in those cases, it is usually more than 10 percent. In this system, known as "pari-mutuel betting," the odds are determined mathematically by the ratio of bets. Most horse racing in the United States, as well as the few remaining greyhound racing and jai alai facilities, use pari-mutuel betting. For any given type of bet (for example, win, place, show, or a trifecta in horse racing), all the money in that type of bet is pooled, and after the house takes its cut, the pool of money is divided among those who bet correctly in proportion to their bet. In pari-mutuel betting, the person laying down a bet does not know what odds he or she will get until the event actually starts, because additional bets affect the size of the pool. Each time someone bets on a horse other than the one you picked, you get a higher payoff if your horse wins. But each time someone bets on your horse, you stand to win less. The house takes no risk, and its cut can be quite high. Churchill Downs, the home of the Kentucky Derby, takes about 20 percent off the top of each betting pool, as do horse tracks in New York State.[5]

You might think you are getting a better deal from the sportsbook in a casino because the casino only takes 10 percent off the top. But unlike the racetracks, casinos and other bookmakers don't simply balance their bets so that they pay out to winners exactly what they take in from losers (minus their cut). They set up the betting markets so that they are, in effect, making bets of their own.

That tactic wouldn't necessarily hurt you if the house were just one more bettor in the market. But the house has way better information than you have, and as in the stock market, better information is worth a fortune in betting markets. You may have worked out an intricate system for betting the NFL games this weekend or think you know when the Reds' starting pitcher looks like he has a gimpy arm, but the house has reams of data on who bets what and how well it pays off. The house knows what people tend to overvalue, such as favorites and big-city teams. Sportsbooks do sometimes lose if a few things line up wrong, as they did on the day of the Browns' missed extra point. But over the long run, bookmakers take the right side of a majority of bets.

Until recently, betting on major professional sports was a bit like drinking during Prohibition: it was technically illegal, but people found a way. Local bookies were often shady guys running solo gambling operations. If a bookie didn't pick up the phone, you were more or less out of luck (though actually better off, since you were likely to lose). But today the sports gambling business is big, getting bigger, and highly sophisticated.

The business has exploded for two reasons—one somewhat dicey from a legal perspective, and the other fully legal (though questionable as public policy). First, like the secondary ticket market, gambling has been revolutionized by the growth of the internet. Online international sportsbooks, like Bovada, Sportsbetting.ag, and 5Dimes, dominate the industry. These sites are able to dodge U.S. restrictions on sports betting by establishing official headquarters offshore (the Caribbean and Central America are popular locations). They can also instill confidence in their legitimacy that the bookie on the phone could never approach. Make a few clicks, enter some credit card information (or, more likely these days, deposit some cryptocurrency), and you're signed up to bet as much as you please, knowing that the site will cash your winnings out at any time you choose. The problem is, if you play longer than a few lucky days, you'll probably have no winnings to cash out.

The second reason sports gambling is growing quickly is that, for municipalities, it is an easy source of revenue. Over the past few decades, state budgets have come to rely more and more on legalized gambling, often in the form of slot machines and blackjack tables in new casinos in cities including Detroit and New Orleans, on riverboats throughout the country, and in lotteries. But the Bradley Act of 1992, named for its chief proponent in the U.S. Senate, New Jersey senator and former NBA star Bill Bradley, prevented any significant expansion of legal sports betting for many years, limiting it to Nevada casinos—and state-sponsored lotteries in Oregon, Delaware, and Montana, where lottery winners are tied to sports game outcomes. But once the Bradley Act was declared unconstitutional by the United States Supreme Court in 2018, it immediately led to an expansion of sports betting at New Jersey and Delaware casinos and, in the 2020 elections, successful referenda to legalize sports betting in Maryland, South Dakota, and Louisiana.

Las Vegas casinos and online sportsbooks offer many forms of betting. For example, matches between two teams can be bet in terms of money lines or point lines. If you want to bet, for instance, on a Seahawks-Vikings game in which the Seahawks are slight favorites, you can either put money on the Seahawks at a -130 money line, which means betting purely on a Seahawks win but at a rate that requires a $1.30 bet for a $1.00 payout, or you can bet on the Seahawks at -2.5, which means that your bet wins if the Seahawks win by more than 2.5 points. If you can't decide which team you like, you can bet the "over" (or the "under"), where the bet pays off if the total points scored by the two teams exceed (or fall short of) some number.

Bookies, like stockbrokers, just make markets in bets. The "prices" (known in this context as "lines") are flexible to reflect bettors' demand and the possibility of receiving new information. If bookies begin taking bets on the Seahawks-Vikings game with the Seahawks as a 2.5-point favorite, and customers are putting $5 on the Vikings for every $1 on the Seahawks, the line will move to correct that disparity; the Seahawks might drop to 1.5-point favorites. Unlike pari-mutuel bettors, however, people who placed their bet when the line was 2.5 points are paid off based on that predetermined line (rather than the 1.5-point line at game time). The line might also move if the bookie receives word that the Seahawks' starting quarterback Russell Wilson will sit out the game, information the bookie is most likely to receive just before most bettors. The adjustments continue until the bookie feels confident about the risk he is assuming on each side.

So why does the bookmaker take a position rather than just balance the bets and keep the 10 percent guaranteed take? Taking all those bets gives bookmakers an information advantage that they can exploit, just like a stock trader with a direct line to a firm's CEO. The casino gets a point spread estimate from its mathematical model, which takes into account past behavior and can generally anticipate which team will be more popular with bettors, then manually adjusts it toward the team that tends to draw more money. The guys that sportsbooks pay to set the lines are some of the most informed and advanced gamblers in the world. Few people can consistently think a step ahead of the bookies (and the vast majority of those who claim they can are lying to you or to themselves). In other words, all but the best gamblers will lose in the long run.

There Are Smarter People Than You

So far, we've discussed two reasons you will lose when you gamble: the house takes a cut, and the house doesn't set fair odds, because it has better information than you have. Now let's add a third factor.

Not only does the house know more than you do, but so do the top gamblers. There are not many of them, but they move a lot of the money in betting markets.

One important bettor, a Berkeley dropout named Bob Stoll—known professionally as Dr. Bob—had a huge impact on the gambling industry. According to the *Wall Street Journal,* sportsbooks were thrown into a panic when Dr. Bob's clients, who paid for an email subscription service that sent them specially recommended weekly football gambling picks, bet millions of dollars a week on a few obscure college games.[6] In his best season, Dr. Bob's NCAA football picks hit at an unbelievable 71 percent; even people who make their living gambling on sports rarely pick at better than 55 or 56 percent. In eight college football seasons from 1999 through 2006, Dr. Bob picked at over 60 percent in four of them, and in only one of those seasons were his picks unprofitable.[7]

Sportsbooks hated Dr. Bob. He was cleaning up at their expense because he had better information than they had. But other bettors (other than those who subscribed to his service) should also have hated Dr. Bob. Dr. Bob was in the same market as casual bettors and taking their money, with the casino acting as middleman. Dr. Bob was the Billy Beane (as in the book and movie *Moneyball*) of NCAA betting. He had a better analysis of the situation than his competitors, and he was able to take advantage of it at the expense of casinos and other bettors.

Just as other teams caught up to Beane's Oakland A's and now have just as much analytical power, so the casinos caught up to Dr. Bob. They hired more analysts and used more computing power to get their line-setting systems up to his standards. Since the end of the 2006 season, Dr. Bob has had decent success picking college football games, but his results no longer blow competitors out of the water. In his eight standout years, he amassed 212.3 "net stars" (a unit he developed to rate himself); in the subsequent seven years, from 2007 to 2013, he added just 13.8 total net stars. That's a drop from 26.54 net stars per season in the first period to 1.97 in the second. His fifth-best season between 1999 and 2006 was more profitable than any year he has had since.

Whatever advanced model that made Dr. Bob so successful was eventually replicated by the bookies' mathematicians. The linemakers were able to build Dr. Bob's clientele into their predictions of what bets would be placed. Dr. Bob was unusually forward about his methods in write-ups on his site (though maybe not as forward as Beane, who gave away his secrets in a book and a movie). Dr. Bob lost the advantage that came with having better information, while the casinos became ever better informed and upped their advantage over regular gamblers.

Well-informed bettors in general (and Dr. Bob in particular) are becoming less of an issue as betting markets get bigger and more sophisticated. So much money has flooded these markets that, like stock markets, they have attracted highly sophisticated people using analytics to seek out even a small opportunity that they can exploit. The bookmakers, in turn, have invested more to stay right behind the smart money. While "touts" like Dr. Bob get hot from time to time, beating the sportsbook as badly or for as long as he did is extremely rare. "Years ago, the technical stuff really worked," Dr. Bob says. "The lines have gotten so much sharper now." But don't worry about Dr. Bob; his real money comes from subscriptions to his newsletters and his website where he reveals his predictions.

If All Else Fails, Cheat

Dr. Bob and the bookmakers make it hard for you to make money because they know more and, in the case of the bookmakers, take some money off the top. But there's yet another group of people out there who are literally stealing your money. It's not news to anyone who has seen *Field of Dreams* or *On the Waterfront* that sports betting markets can be manipulated. When that happens, the loser isn't the bookmaker, if it managed the line properly; it's the uninformed bettors who did not know what was going on—that is, you and me.

The gentlemanly country-club sport of tennis has been a center of match fixing in recent years. Almost every day, professional matches all over the world pit good but unknown players with world rankings in the hundreds or thousands against one another. Betting sites will take bets on these matches, and sometimes the bets are more specific than simply who will win the match. For example, in 2016, the Australian tennis player Oliver Anderson reached a world ranking of 639, which is the best he has ever done. That October, he played his fellow Australian Harrison Lombe, who was ranked 1,634th in the world and was not expected to give Anderson much of a match. Before the match, CrownBet—an Australian betting site—was offering to take bets that Lombe would win the first set. However, the site refused to take a $10,000 (Australian dollars) bet because it was suspicious. It did accept a bet of $2,000.[8]

Anderson, who was the reigning Australian Open Boys' champion at the time, lost the first set 6–4 before wiping out Lombe 6–0, 6–2, and winning the match. He later admitted to accepting money to throw the first set.

This minor scandal raises two questions. The first one—the easy one—is why Anderson would accept this payment. His incentives were pretty strong. At the time he was suspended for match fixing, he had amassed career earnings of about $20,000. That is not nearly enough to cover the expenses of being a touring professional, much less to live on. It certainly cannot support the luxurious lifestyle of Roger Federer, but it is typical for a tennis pro who is well outside the

WHO WINS WHEN PEOPLE GAMBLE?

world top 100. A few hundred dollars here and a thousand dollars there to drop a set (or even a match) from time to time can be a strong temptation when that money means a decent hotel room or a good meal or even just staying afloat on tour while hoping to break through.

The harder question to answer is why in the world does Crown-Bet (the Australian betting site) take bets on who will win the first set of some match that nobody beyond the players and their mothers cares about? Who would bet on those matches if they were *not* fixed? Nobody cared whether Anderson or Lombe won. The match had all the hallmarks of a bad market for regular bettors (that is, those who are not cheaters with inside information), given that there was not much money in the betting pool, the players were vulnerable to financial inducements to throw the match, and it is pretty easy to drop a set on purpose. The Wimbledon finals (or pretty much any match in a tournament offering serious prize money) are a lot less likely to put uninformed bettors at a big disadvantage, because the players have too much to lose in prize and endorsement money to risk being caught throwing a match. CrownBet must set the odds with a large vig (that is, so that its expected take is very high), because otherwise the company could never make a profit setting a market on matches so prone to fixing.

A much larger betting market than the lowest reaches of professional tennis is college basketball. People bet large sums in Vegas casinos and other legal venues, as well as illegally with bookies, on NCAA games. For both coaches and players, winning games has a major effect on their futures, so the costs of throwing a game are extremely high. But maybe a smart player can figure out how to win the game and win a bet at the same time.

College basketball might be an easy sport to fix: the players are young, impressionable, and often from poor backgrounds; a place on the team might be the most high-leverage position some players ever hold; and it only takes paying off one or two players to have substantial control over outcomes. Also, like tennis players who throw a set but win the match, basketball players on heavily favored teams can lose against the spread while winning the game—a practice known as "point shaving." Imagine, for example, that Michigan is favored by thirty-three points against Binghamton (an actual recent spread). Michigan can coast to a twenty-point win while those who know the game is fixed can bet that Michigan will not cover the spread.

The economist Justin Wolfers analyzed the outcomes of more than forty-four thousand NCAA games and concluded that point shaving is fairly common. Although subsequent studies have cast doubt on some details of his findings, college basketball has a long history of fixed games as young, unpaid athletes sought to cash in on what might be their best moneymaking opportunities. For example, in 1997, Arizona State guard Steven Smith employed the "win but don't cover" strategy quite successfully for a few games before ultimately ending up in prison.[9]

The bottom line is that, in many sporting events, someone actually in the game has better information than you do. In at least a few games, that person may be using it to bet on himself (as Pete Rose famously did) or to fix the outcome. But either way, "smart money" (that is, the people who know how a game is fixed) will win out against regular bettors, so you might be out some money before the game you bet on even starts.

Should Sports Betting Be Legal?

If your goal is to make money, betting on sports is a fool's errand. You might have a good day from time to time. But in the end, you will lose. The bookmakers take a cut, other people in the betting market have better information than you do, and some of them are cheating. The financial return on betting is so lousy that some people might conclude that all sports betting should be illegal because it's just a way for a few businesses to take money from naive fans.

But let's slow down and take the arguments for a ban on sports betting one at a time. One argument is that gambling lowers productivity. People spend time at work gambling, with the NCAA's March Madness and Super Bowl pools often cited as particular distractions. One survey showed that March Madness bracket activities ranked third among "tech-related office distractions" (behind Facebook and texting); the authors of another study estimated that March Madness lowers U.S. productivity by $6.3 billion each year. This argument does not get you very far, though, because other studies suggest that March Madness activities increase office morale.[10] Wasted time is a real concern, but not enough to demand policy interventions.

Another argument is that gambling is unfair, for all the reasons I noted earlier. More-informed bettors take money from less-informed bettors, both legally and illegally. That is true in the stock market, as well, and nobody (well, few people) would outlaw stock markets. Some stock investors have better information because they do better research. Others have inside information, though it's technically illegal to use it. However, the stock market, unlike sports betting markets, is an important financial tool that allows companies to raise capital and creates incentives for executives to manage companies well. Stock markets are unfair and cause problems—and therefore require regulation (arguably more than they currently get)—but they serve a purpose: they make the whole economy work better.

Sports gambling confers no such society-wide benefit. Or does it? Remember that gambling brings people utility—they enjoy it. As long as gamblers are reasonably informed about the disadvantages they face in the betting market, there's no reason not to let them spend their money on gambling, just as society lets people spend their money on clothes, furniture, and sports paraphernalia.

Indeed, if all gamblers gambled for fun and could afford the bets they made, then the answer would be easy. Sports betting should be legal, and the market would set the odds for each contest. But the best argument for banning sports betting centers on a small set of the betting population: gambling addicts.

Addiction to gambling destroys lives. There's no way around it. Statistics are hard to come by, but there are many cases of gambling-related suicide.[11] Most estimates put the number of people with pathological gambling problems at 0.5 to 1 percent of the population in most Western countries, though many of those people are addicted to nonsports gambling. Almost all problem gamblers are men.

From a policy perspective, it should (in principle) be relatively easy to decide whether to legalize sports betting. Society just needs to decide if the dramatic costs to the problem-gambling population and their families outweigh the benefits of gambling to the much larger responsible-gambling public. While one could imagine banning sports betting on that basis, doing so becomes less realistic when you consider that many problem gamblers will still gamble if it is illegal. They might even be made worse off, because they would now owe money to shady bookies instead of casinos, or they might just sit at home and gamble illegally over the internet. Making gambling easier to access increases the number of problem gamblers, but not necessarily by a lot. Studies show that people who live near casinos are more likely to be problem gamblers, for example, but the effect is not dramatic, and it is possible that people who choose to live near casinos are more prone to problem gambling to begin with.[12]

Perhaps the best argument against outlawing sports (and other) betting comes from the historical example of Prohibition, which banned liquor sales in the United States from 1920 to 1933. Even though it lowered the total amount of liquor consumed, Prohibition also resulted in liquor production and distribution being controlled by a costly and destabilizing criminal element. Moreover, the people whose consumption was most dramatically lowered were the casual and social drinkers for whom drinking did not create significant problems. Addicts found a way to drink, often getting sick on unregulated booze in the process. By the same logic, serious gamblers are likely to gamble even if it is illegal. Banning gambling will most affect casual gamblers for whom the benefits are relatively high (or for whom the costs are low) while not necessarily stopping the problem gamblers, who will still seek out bookies and other unsavory betting mediums.

In the end, therefore, I don't think there is a credible case for outlawing sports gambling. But can we make legal sports gambling less damaging? It may not make a big difference, but it seems sensible to at least insist that all gambling-related advertising be realistic and show winners and losers in their proper proportions. Ads for casinos and racetracks (as well as nonsports gambling ads for lotteries and the like) invariably show people celebrating after winning some money. But most people lose. So we might benefit from a law that says, if you want to show people celebrating their winnings, you have to show even more people going home disappointed.

The country of Singapore, not known for its progressive social policies, uses an innovative method to keep people from gambling if they cannot afford it. Casinos in Singapore will happily let any adult foreigner enter. It would be illogical to charge foreigners to gamble, given all the other destinations they can choose to visit. But residents have to pay 150 Singapore dollars (about $110 U.S.) to enter a casino for a day, or 3,000 Singapore dollars for an annual pass.[13] This system creates a nice source of revenue for the government and dissuades people with less money from gambling. Singapore undid some of this policy's advantages, however, by allowing residents to use two online

gambling sites without a minimum payment (which makes one wonder if Singapore is fine with letting poor people gamble but just doesn't
want them doing it in sight of tourists).[14] Still, charging people fixed
fees to be allowed to gamble is a potentially useful way to lower compulsive and spontaneous gambling—though it does nothing to deter
addictive gambling by people rich enough to pay the entry fee.

One optimistic take on the rise of sports gambling is that it is a
sign of overall increases in wealth. Most sports bets are simply expenditures on leisure activity, like buying a ticket to a movie or going to a
restaurant. These expenditures become possible as societies get richer.
When most people are worried about survival, they don't spend
money on gambling and other leisure goods (though, again, it is important to keep in mind problem gamblers). So even though purist
sports fans may prefer games without betting, sports bets are likely
here to stay, and even though many more socially useful ways exist
for people to spend their money, there is nothing wrong with people
enjoying themselves.

Epilogue

Sometimes the connection between sports and economics is simple, direct, and obvious. But only after the fact.

Real Madrid has been one of the world's most successful soccer teams for more than a century, both financially and on the field. In 2000, Florentino Perez took over as president of the team while continuing to run Spain's largest construction company.

Perez, a very wealthy man, saw a way to grow his soccer club to even greater heights. In the United States, major sports leagues such as the NBA and MLB have a constant and relatively small set of teams that play only against one another. These top leagues get the vast majority of TV airtime and fan attention, and they bring in revenue that dwarfs any other league in their respective sports. European soccer, on the other hand, comprises hundreds of teams in a loose collection of leagues, with talent spread out more evenly across all of them. Perez led an effort to build a "Super League" on the apparently sensible premise that if his league could assemble the best teams from across Europe, it could sell broadcast rights for huge amounts. By emulating an American sports league, the Super League would get the lion's share of fan attention, broadcasting time, and revenue. As the richest soccer league, it would inevitably accumulate the best players. Its dominance would be self-sustaining.

The business model was simple: bring together the best teams to play each other regularly. The best players would face off more often, and there would be fewer mismatches between top-level teams and local squads with lower budgets. Fans would pay the most to see top teams playing each other. And indeed, if the owners had been starting European professional soccer from scratch, the Super League would probably have been a huge success.

After years of planning, Real Madrid and eleven other top European teams announced the formation of the Super League in the spring of 2021. Perez and the league's other backers knew contracts and business, but it turns out they didn't know economics very well. They ignored the economic value of tradition and underestimated the potential backlash from local fans, politicians, and others whose favorite teams, no longer playing against the best competition, would be overshadowed by the Super League. Many politicians condemned the Super League, including British prime minister Boris Johnson. This outcome was entirely predictable. Although the league would have been great for the players and owners of a few top teams, far more would have been poorer, and most fans would have been less happy. Johnson and his party count on votes from the whole population.

Within two days of being announced with great fanfare, the Super League collapsed. Perez and his colleagues had misread the market. The market almost always wins.

Notes

Prologue

1. Aaron Dodson, "On This Day in NBA Finals History: Steve Kerr's 17-Foot Jumper Clinches Bulls' 1997 Title," *The Undefeated*, June 13, 2017.

2. "CERA: The New EPO Discovered at the Tour de France," *Cycling Weekly*, July 17, 2008; "Rashid Ramzi Stripped of Beijing Olympic 1500m Gold After Failing Dope Test," *The Telegraph*, November 18, 2009.

3. "Lee6 Wins U.S. Women's Open, Pockets $1M," Associated Press, June 2, 2019.

Chapter 1. Should You Help Your Kid Become a Pro Athlete?

1. Bradley T. Ewing, "The Labor Market Effects of High School Sports Participation: Evidence from Wage and Fringe Benefit Differentials," *Journal of Sports Economics* 8 (2007): 255–265.

2. Michael Lechner, "Long-Run Labour Market and Health Effects of Individual Sports Activities," *Journal of Health Economics* 28 (2009): 839–854.

3. Michael B. Ransom and Tyler Ransom, "Do High School Sports Build or Reveal Character? Bounding Causal Estimates of Sports Participation," *Economics of Education Review* 64 (2018): 75–89.

4. Natural Resources Defense Council, www.nrdc.org, December 31, 2015.

5. Edward B. Fiske, "Gaining Admission: Athletes Win Preference," *New York Times*, January 7, 2001.

6. Thomas J. Espenshade, Chang Y. Chung, and Joan L. Walling, "Admission Preferences for Minority Students, Athletes, and Legacies at Elite Universities," *Social Science Quarterly* 85 (December 2004).

7. Full disclosure: I am a Middlebury graduate. But various college rankings have considered Middlebury more prestigious than these other schools.

8. I am only considering legitimate athletic scholarships, not the type given

by the Stanford sailing coach and others exposed during the 2019 "Varsity Blues" scandal.

9. "Average per Athlete 2020," www.scholarshipstats.com/average-per-athlete.html; "Athletic Scholarships: Everything You Need to Know," www.ncsasports.org/recruiting/how-to-get-recruited/scholarship-facts; "Scholarships," www.ncaa.org/student-athletes/future/scholarships; Hanna Muniz, "How Many College Students Are in the U.S.?" www.bestcolleges.com/blog/how-many-college-students-in-the-us/. One percent is based on 200,000 as a fraction of 20 million college students. All sites accessed April 23, 2021.

10. Bryce Druzin, "The Cardinal Connection: Why Joining Stanford's Football Team Is a Great Career Move," *San Jose Business Journal,* August 11, 2014; Paul Wachter, "Wall Street's Lacrosse Mafia," *Bloomberg Business,* March 22, 2012.

11. David Card, "Using Geographic Variation in College Proximity to Estimate the Return to Schooling," Working Paper, National Bureau of Economic Research, 1993; Orley Ashenfelter and Alan Krueger, "Estimates of the Economic Return to Schooling from a New Sample of Twins," *American Economic Review* 84 (1994): 1157–1173; Joshua D. Angrist and Alan B. Krueger, "Does Compulsory School Attendance Affect Schooling and Earnings?" *Quarterly Journal of Economics* 106 (1991): 979–1014.

12. "Kevin Durant Biography Facts, Childhood and Personal Life," storytell.com, accessed June 6, 2021; Sam Anderson, "Kevin Durant and (Possibly) the Best Basketball Team of All Time," *New York Times Magazine,* June 2, 2021.

13. It's important to note that the statistical focus on Durant's race is not ideal, as other (possibly more important) factors are correlated with race and limit someone with Durant's background. For example, having a single mother and being poor are likely to be more important than race. I use race because the data are reliable and compelling. But note that individual circumstances beyond race should drive the calculation of whether or not to focus on sports at a young age.

14. African American wage and employment information from quarterly releases by the U.S. Bureau of Labor Statistics; latest version available at www.bls.gov/news.release/pdf/wkyeng.pdf; Raj Chetty, Nathaniel Hendren, Maggie R. Jones, and Sonya R. Porter, "Race and Economic Opportunity in the United States: An Intergenerational Perspective," *Quarterly Journal of Economics* 135 (2020): 711–1014.

15. David Wharton, "Sweet Youth," *Los Angeles Times,* March 18, 2007.

16. Charles Nuamah, "Tall NBA Players Who Had Relatively Short Parents," howtheyplay.com, accessed June 6, 2021.

17. Calculations based on the height calculator at Tall.Life, https://tall.life/height
-percentile-calculator-age-country, accessed April 23, 2021.

18. Jonny Hughes, "Top 15 Little-Known Facts About Kevin Durant," *The-Sportster*, December 24, 2014. The first pick in that NBA draft, Greg Oden, was a very sad story. Because of recurring injuries, Oden has never played in the NBA for any sustained period of time. But all the calculations for Durant apply to Oden, who was also born in 1988 and made millions of dollars in guaranteed NBA contracts despite being unable to play.

19. I look at income statistics for Black men born in 1988 using a representative sample from the U.S. Census Bureau's American Community Survey. This huge survey is widely used by social scientists, as well as by federal and local government to allocate many billions of dollars of funds each year.

20. Emmanuel Saez and Gabriel Zucman, "Wealth Inequality in the United States Since 1913: Evidence from Capitalized Income Tax Data," *Quarterly Journal of Economics* 131, no. 2 (2016).

21. Two other professions where men often earn large incomes at relatively young ages are acting and music. I did not find anyone born in 1988 making an eight-figure salary in either of these fields or any other field.

22. Chris Palmer, "From the Bottom to the Top: The Russell Westbrook Story," *Bleacher Report*, November 12, 2015.

23. Seth Stephens-Davidowitz, "In the N.B.A., Zip Code Matters," *New York Times*, November 2, 2013.

24. Brook Larmer, "Golf in China Is Younger Than Tiger Woods, but Growing Up Fast," *New York Times*, July 11, 2013.

Chapter 2. What Do Silicon Valley and Czech Women's Tennis Have in Common?

1. Calculations based on medal counts and populations from www.medals percapita.com/ as of March 20, 2018.

2. The sports are Alpine (downhill) skiing (combined ranking for all events), archery, badminton, bowling, golf, judo (the heaviest weight class for each gender), kayak (one kilometer), marathon, modern pentathlon, Nordic (cross-country) skiing, short track speed skating (1,500 meter), skeleton, swimming (400-meter individual medley), table tennis, tennis, and trampoline. Rankings were collected in the latter part of 2015.

3. Matthew Futterman and Kevin Helliker, "The Mystery of Norway," *Wall Street Journal,* February 24, 2010.

4. "Joy of Sport—for All: Sport Policy Document, 2011–2015," Norges Idrettsforbund, 2015, www.sportanddev.org/sites/default/files/downloads/sportpolicydocument2011_2015_1.pdf.

5. Norwegian Olympic and Paralympic Committee and Confederation of Sports (NIF), www.idrettsforbundet.no/english/.

6. Elsa Kristiansen and Barrie Houlihan, "Developing Young Athletes: The Role of Private Sport Schools in the Norwegian Sport System," *International Review of the Sociology of Sport* 52 (2017): 447–469.

7. Marathon rankings from www.all-athletics.com, which are no longer available there.

8. Unlike PAPIs, which are calculated for each country in a sport, Herfindahl indexes are calculated to measure the concentration for the top 25 as a group.

9. Gregory Warner, "How One Kenyan Tribe Produces the World's Best Runners," National Public Radio, November 1, 2013.

10. Jackie Dikos, "The Simple Staple," *Runner's World,* June 28, 2012; Warner, "How One Kenyan Tribe"; Max Fisher, "Why Kenyans Make Such Great Runners: A Story of Genes and Cultures," *The Atlantic,* April 17, 2012; Brendan Koerner, "Why Are Kenyans Fast Runners?" Slate.com, 2003.

11. Warner, "How One Kenyan Tribe."

12. Adharanand Finn, "Kenya's Marathon Men," *The Guardian,* April 8, 2012.

13. "Czechoslovakia Strives to Maintain Tennis Tradition," AP Story, December 21, 1985.

14. Sarah Pileggi, "Fanatics and Fools," *Sports Illustrated,* January 12, 1981.

15. John Branch, "Czech Women Continue Wimbledon Onslaught," *New York Times,* June 30, 2014.

16. "Czechoslovakia Strives to Maintain Tennis Tradition," AP Story, December 21, 1985.

17. Pileggi, "Fanatics and Fools."

18. Petra Kvitova's bio, http://petrakvitova.net/petra/, accessed May 24, 2019.

19. "Petra Kvitova: Martina Navratilova," Tennis.com, December 2, 2015, www.tennis.com/pro-game/2015/12/petra-kvitova-martina-navratilova/56930.

20. This particular survey sampled eleven nations, including Hong Kong, Germany, Italy, Belgium, and Portugal.

21. The OECD has thirty-four members, including virtually all of western Europe plus most of the rest of the world's developed countries.

22. *The Global Gender Gap Report,* World Economic Forum, 2020; "Iceland Leads the Way to Women's Equality in the Workplace," *The Economist,* March 4, 2020.

23. OECD, "Saving Rate," https://data.oecd.org/natincome/saving-rate.htm.

24. Pay gap from OECD, https://data.oecd.org/earnwage/gender-wage-gap.htm, accessed September 19, 2021.

25. Official World Golf Ranking, www.owgr.com/ranking; Rolex Women's World Golf Rankings, www.rolexrankings.com/rankings.

26. Randall Mell, "Pak's Influence on Game Immeasurable," *Golf Central* blog, www.golfchannel.com/news/golftalkcentral/paks-influence-game-immeasurable/.

27. Alan Shipnuck, "A Seminal Win at the 1998 U.S. Women's Open Has Triggered Nearly Two Decades of South Korean Dominance on the LPGA Tour," *NCGA Golf,* Summer 2015.

Chapter 3. Why Do Athletes Cheat and Lie?

1. McGwire has since admitted to regular steroid use throughout his career, and Sosa's name was leaked from an infamous confidential list of positive drug tests in the early 2000s.

2. Benjamin Soloway, "Scandal on the Tour de France," *Foreign Policy,* July 3, 2015.

3. Of course, if the prisoners are friends and legitimately care about each other's welfare, they might help each other out. The athletes I focus on, however, are likely to be more like the self-interested actors in economic models, given the importance of winning relative to any other outcome.

4. David Walsh, *From Lance to Landis* (Ballantine Books, 2007), 66.

5. Walsh, *From Lance to Landis,* 69.

6. United States Anti-doping Agency, "Report on Proceedings Under the World Anti-doping Code and the USADA Protocol, United States Anti-doping Agency vs. Lance Armstrong," August 24, 2012, www.usada.org/wp-content/uploads/Reasoned Decision.pdf.

7. Dick Marty, Peter Nicholson, and Ulrich Haas, "Cycling Independent Reform Commission, Report to the President of the Union Cycliste Internationale," 2015.

8. FanGraphs' "wins above replacement" (WAR) measure, for instance, gives Bonds's 1998 season an 8.5 rating, tied with McGwire and far exceeding Sosa's 7.1. Baseball Reference WAR gives Bonds an 8.1, McGwire a 7.5, and Sosa a 6.4.

9. Nate Silver, "Lies, Damned Lies: The Steroid Game," *Baseball Prospectus,* May 7, 2009.

10. Suzanne Massie taught President Ronald Reagan this phrase, which he made famous. The phrase had a rebirth in 2015 during negotiation of the Iran nuclear deal. See Barton Swaim, "'Trust but Verify': An Untrustworthy Political Phrase," *Washington Post,* March 11, 2016.

11. Jennifer Laaser and John Fauber, "Baseball's Drug Testing: Thorough or Easily Thwarted?" *Milwaukee Journal Sentinel,* July 14, 2013, http://archive.jsonline.com /news/health/up-to-20-major-league-players-to-be-suspended-but-not-because-of -stringent-tests-b99391321-215413631.html.

12. J. Savulescu, B. Foddy, and M. Clayton, "Why We Should Allow Performance Enhancing Drugs in Sports," *British Journal of Sports Medicine* 38 (2004).

13. In fairness to Lewis, that test might truly have been a case of inadvertent use, as he claimed: the relatively low stimulant levels that triggered the positive result would not be considered high enough to fail the test by today's standards.

14. John Brant, "The Marriage That Led to the Russian Track Team's Olympic Ban," *New York Times Magazine,* June 22, 2016. Focusing on doping by a middle-distance woman, this article suggests that doping lowers the best times of women in the 800 meters by at least five seconds, or 4 percent. Four percent for a 100-meter dash is about .38 seconds. Some extremely unreliable guesses suggest 0.2 second savings from steroids for top 100-meter sprinters.

15. In the summer of 2018, the American newcomer Christopher Coleman ran a 9.79-second 100 meters. The fastest 100 meters by someone other than Usain Bolt with a long history of running and testing with no positive tests is the 9.82 by Richard Thompson of Trinidad and Tobago.

16. Oliver Pickup, "Usain Bolt Denies Using Performance-Enhancing Drugs Ahead of Paris Diamond League Meeting," *The Telegraph,* July 3, 2013, www.telegraph .co.uk/sport/othersports/athletics/10157145/Usain-Bolt-denies-using-performance -enhancing-drugs-ahead-of-Paris-Diamond-League-meeting.html.

17. For the Armstrong denial quotes, see Stephen McMillan, "Lance Armstrong's Doping Denials—in Quotes," *The Guardian,* January 18, 2013, www.theguardian .com/sport/2013/jan/18/lance-armstrong-doping-denials-quotes.

18. Charlie Gillis, "Too Fast to Be Clean: Why the World's Fastest Man Can't

Run Clear of Controversy," *Maclean's*, September 1, 2009, www.macleans.ca/society /too-fast-to-be-clean/.

19. On the use of steroids in swimming, see Donald McRae, "Michael Jamieson: 'Swimming Has a Problem. Micro-dosing Is a Huge Issue,'" *The Guardian*, January 28, 2018; in soccer, Ferdinand Dyck, "An Ex-Pro Soccer Player Explains How Easy It Is to Dope," *Vice*, July 6, 2018; in skiing, Gordy Megroz, "Lindsey Vonn and the (Vast) Potential for Doping in Ski Racing," *Outside*, June 5, 2013.

Chapter 4. Are Athletes Worth All That Money?

1. U.S. Bureau of Labor Statistics, "Economic News Release," table 1, www.bls .gov/news.release/wkyeng.to1.htm, accessed June 13, 2021.

2. MLB from "Scherzer Highest-Paid Player, Red Sox Top Payroll List Again," Associated Press, March 28, 2019; NBA from "2020–21 Player Contracts," Basketball Reference, www.basketball-reference.com/contracts/players.html. When quoting statistics on pay for a typical worker or athlete, I use medians wherever possible, because the U.S. Census Bureau reports medians in most cases, and because medians give a better sense of the typical person, while averages can be skewed by a few outliers. I could not find median pay for European soccer leagues, but the averages there are also in the multi-millions of dollars.

3. "Sports List of the Day," December 5, 2011, https://sportslistoftheday.com /2011/12/05/major-league-baseballs-average-salaries-1964–2010/. Only average (as opposed to median) salaries are available for the 1960s, so I can only provide an upper bound based on the fact that averages in sports salaries tend to be higher than medians.

4. United States Census Bureau, "Current Population Reports: Consumer Income," September 24, 1965, www2.census.gov/prod2/popscan/p60-047.pdf, accessed June 13, 2021.

5. Jabari Young, "Major League Baseball Revenue for 2019 Season Hits a Record $10.7 Billion," CNBC; James Wagner, "M.L.B. Extends TV Deal with Fox Sports Through 2028," November 15, 2018; Maury Brown, "MLB Sees Record Revenues of $10.3 Billion for 2018," January 7, 2019, Forbes.com.

6. Shalini Ramachandran, "MLB's Streaming-Tech Unit Goes Pro," *Wall Street Journal*, February 23, 2015.

7. Dave Cameron, "Big Ticket Signings Don't Drive Attendance," FanGraphs .com, December 9, 2011.

8. Gerald W. Scully, "Pay and Performance in Major League Baseball," *Ameri-

can Economic Review 64 (1971); Henry Aaron Baseball Reference page, accessed December 14, 2020.

9. Matt Swartz, "The Recent History of Free Agent Signings," FanGraphs.com, July 11, 2017.

10. Michael Haupert, "MLB's Annual Salary Leaders Since 1874," Society for American Baseball Research, http://sabr.org/research/mlbs-annual-salary-leaders-1874-2012.

11. Marc Topkin, "Tommy Pham Wins Arbitration Case over Rays, Gets $4.1M," *Tampa Bay Times,* February 5, 2019.

12. Sherwin Rosen and Allen Sanderson, "Labour Markets in Professional Sports," *Economic Journal* III (2001).

13. Hayley C. Cuccinello, "The World's Highest-Paid Comedians of 2018," Forbes.com, December 19, 2018.

14. *Federal Baseball Club v. National League,* 259 U.S. 200 (1922).

15. Simon Rottenberg, "The Baseball Players' Labor Market," *Journal of Political Economy* 64 (1956).

16. Haupert, "MLB's Annual Salary Leaders Since 1874."

17. Emmanuel Saez, "Income and Wealth Inequality: Evidence and Policy Implications," Neubauer Collegium Lecture, University of Chicago, 2014.

18. Kevin J. Murphy, "Executive Compensation: Where We Are, and How We Got Here," in *Handbook of the Economics of Finance,* edited by George M. Constantinides, Milton Harris, and Rene M. Stulz (Elsevier, 2013).

19. Steven N. Kaplan and Joshua Rauh, "It's the Market: The Broad-Based Rise in the Return to Top Talent," *Journal of Economics Perspectives* (2013).

20. Benjamin Kabak, "The Economics of Yankee Tickets," River Avenue Blues, March 14, 2008, http://riveraveblues.com/2008/03/the-economics-of-yankee-tickets-2327/.

21. "New York Yankee Suites," Suite Experience Group, www.suiteexperiencegroup.com/all-suites/mlb/new-york-yankees/, accessed May 24, 2019.

22. Tadd Haislop, "Patrick Mahomes Contract Details: Here's How Much Guaranteed Money Chiefs QB Will Make in 'Half-Billion' Dollar Deal," *Sporting News,* September 10, 2020.

23. Debra Bell, "*US News* Questioned Football's Future Nearly 45 Years Ago," *US News and World Report,* February 1, 2013.

24. I use Mahomes as an example because of his huge contract. That he does ads for an insurance company is a happy coincidence.

25. Dave Cameron, "Big Ticket Signings Don't Drive Attendance," FanGraphs .com, December 9, 2011; Craig Edwards, "Mike Trout Leaves Money on the Table Again," FanGraphs.com, March 19, 2019.

26. Ross Tucker, "No Guarantees in the NFL," July 6, 2016, www.sportson earth.com/article/188169010/guaranteed-contracts-will-not-work-nfl.

27. I have focused on baseball and football because the contract forms lie at opposite ends of the risk-versus-incentive spectrums. Basketball contracts look closer to MLB contracts in that they are fully guaranteed, but they are shorter than the longest MLB deals because of restrictions imposed by the collective bargaining arrangement between the NBA and its players' union. NHL contracts also tend to be fully guaranteed and can be long-term. The classic study of "shirking" by athletes is Kenneth Lehn, "Property Rights, Risk Sharing and Player Disability in Major League Baseball," *Journal of Law and Economics* 25 (1982). Other baseball studies find less moral hazard, including Anthony C. Krautmann, "Shirking or Stochastic Productivity in Major League Baseball?" *Southern Economic Journal* 56 (1990). On soccer, see Bernard Frick, "Performance, Salaries, and Contract Length: Empirical Evidence from German Soccer," *International Journal of Sport Finance* 6 (2011); on the NBA, see David J. Berri and Anthony C. Krautmann, "Shirking on the Court: Testing for the Incentive Effects of Guaranteed Pay," *Economic Inquiry* 44 (2006).

28. This estimate is based on comparing actual NBA revenues in the lockout-shortened 2011–2012 season to the average of 2010–2011 and 2012–2013 NBA revenues. See "National Basketball Association Total League Revenue from 2001/02 to 2019/20," Statista.com, www.statista.com/statistics/193467/total-league-revenue-of -the-nba-since-2005/, accessed June 8, 2021. An alternative estimate, from *Forbes,* is that the total losses to the NBA and players were $800 million. See Patrick Rishe, "NBA Lockout Costs League $800 Million . . . and Counting; Players Justified to Fight in Courts," Forbes.com, November 16, 2011.

Chapter 5. Why Do Athletes Use
Their Least Successful Moves So Often?

1. Adding the shoot-straight option for the kicker and the don't-dive option for the goalie makes things more complicated, but the logic remains exactly the same.

2. Left is the natural side for a right-footed kicker to aim and is, indeed, a consistently better bet for right-footed kickers. The opposite holds true for left-footed kickers.

3. Ignacio Palacios-Huerta, "Professionals Play Minimax," *Review of Economic Studies* 70 (2003): 395–415.

4. That's only 30 percent of the time rather than one-third—close enough for me, especially given that my optimal percentage of one-third was obtained somewhat arbitrarily.

5. I did not use this example in my case, because I aim for the center of the box on every serve and let general inaccuracy generate the random strategy.

6. Mark Walker and John Wooders, "Minimax Play at Wimbledon," *American Economic Review* 91, no. 5 (2001): 1521–1538.

7. Shih-Hsun Hsu, Chen-Ying Huang, and Cheng-Tao Tang, "Minimax Play at Wimbledon: Comment," *American Economic Review* 97, no. 1 (2007): 517–523.

8. Kudos to the astute readers who have figured out that my stopwatch method actually introduces a small amount of serial dependence in my serve-and-volley strategy. A truly random strategy would have me serve and volley an *average* of three times every ten points, but the stopwatch method means that I serve and volley *exactly* three out of every ten points.

9. Axel Anderson, Jeremy Rosen, John Rust, Kin-Ping Wong, "Disequilibrium Plan in Tennis," working paper, February 2021.

10. Neil Paine, "Game Theory Says R. A. Dickey Should Throw More Knuckleballs," FiveThirtyEight.com, August 13, 2015.

11. Matt Swartz, "Bayes at the Plate: Game Theory and Pitch Selection," 2013 SABR Analytics Conference Presentation, http://sabr.org/latest/2013-sabr-analytics-conference-research-presentations, accessed July 3, 2014. Interview with Matt Swartz on July 13, 2014.

12. Mike Matheny, "Calling Pitches," blog post, www.mikematheny.com/mikes-blog/calling-pitches, accessed July 5, 2014.

Chapter 6. How Does Discrimination Lead to a Proliferation of French Canadian Goalies?

1. Alexander Wolff, "The NFL's Jackie Robinson," *Sports Illustrated,* October 12, 2009.

2. Timothy Burke, "Your Complete Quotable Guide to Decades of Donald Sterling's Racism," *Deadspin,* April 26, 2014.

3. For a high-stakes example of the problems caused by statistical discrimination, see Mike Baker and Nicholas Bogel-Burroughs, "How a Common Air Freshener Can Result in a High-Stakes Traffic Stop," *New York Times,* April 17, 2021.

4. Joseph Price and Justin Wolfers, "Racial Discrimination Among NBA Referees," *Quarterly Journal of Economics* 125 (2010): 1859–1887.

5. Jerry Zgoda and Dennis Brackin, "Timberwolves: Pale in Comparison to Rest of NBA," *Minneapolis Star Tribune,* October 28, 2012.

6. Howard Sinker, "Recalling Calvin Griffith's Bigoted Outburst in Southern Minnesota," *Minneapolis Star Tribune,* April 30, 2014.

7. *Hang Up and Listen* podcast, "The Major League Baseball Needs to Reckon with the Negro Leagues Edition," August 17, 2020.

8. "1965 NBA All-Star Game," Basketball Reference, www.basketball-reference.com/allstar/NBA_1965.html, accessed June 10, 2021; "1975 All-Star Game Voting," Basketball Reference, www.basketball-reference.com/allstar/NBA_1975_voting.html, accessed June 10, 2021; growth in black players, 1954–1970, Gerald W. Scully, "Economic Discrimination in Professional Sports," *Law and Contemporary Problems* 38 (1973): 67–84.

9. Scully, "Economic Discrimination in Professional Sports"; Lawrence M. Kahn and Peter D. Sherer, "Racial Differences in Professional Basketball Players' Compensation," *Journal of Labor Economics* 6 (1988): 40–61; Lawrence M. Kahn, "The Sports Business as a Labor Market Laboratory," *Journal of Economic Perspectives* 14 (2000): 75–94.

10. Mark T. Kanazawa and Jonas P. Funk, "Racial Discrimination in Professional Basketball: Evidence from Nielsen Ratings," *Economic Inquiry* 39 (2001): 599–608.

11. Frank Newport, "In U.S., 87% Approve of Black-White Marriage, vs. 4% in 1958," Gallup.com, July 25, 2013.

12. Ha Hoang and Daniel A. Rascher, "The NBA, Exit Discrimination, and Career Earnings," *Industrial Relations: A Journal of Economy and Society* 31 (1999): 69–91; Peter A. Groothuis and J. Richard Hill, "Exit Discrimination in the NBA: A Duration Analysis of Career Length," *Economic Inquiry* 42 (2004): 341–349.

13. Stefan Szymanski, "A Market Test for Discrimination in the English Professional Soccer Leagues," *Journal of Political Economy* 108 (2000): 590–603.

14. For example, the reaction by Boston Bruins fans after losing a playoff game in 2014 on an overtime goal by star Montreal Canadiens defenseman P. K. Subban, who is of African Caribbean descent. Bruins supporters on Twitter used Subban's name and the n-word in conjunction more than seventeen thousand times in the hours after the goal. "P. K. Subban Targeted by Racist Tweets After Habs Win," CBC News, May 2, 2014.

15. Philip Authier, "The Dream of Independence Lives on in a New Generation," *Montreal Gazette,* October 24, 2020.

16. Marc Lavoie, Gilles Grenier, and Serge Coulombe, "Discrimination and Performance Differentials in the National Hockey League," *Canadian Public Policy* 13 (1987): 407–422.

17. W. Bentley MacLeod, "Optimal Contracting with Subjective Evaluation," *American Economic Review* 93 (2003): 216–240.

18. Alan Schwarz, "Study of NBA Sees Racial Bias in Calling Fouls," *New York Times,* May 2, 2007, A1.

19. Devin G. Pope, Joseph Price, and Justin Wolfers, "Awareness Reduces Racial Bias," *Management Science* 64 (2018): 4988–4995; "Ref, You Suck!" *Against the Rules with Michael Lewis* podcast, April 2, 2019.

20. It's necessary to distinguish "African American" (or, more specifically, U.S. born with African heritage) from "Black" here, as many major leaguers of African descent were born in Latin America.

21. Major League Baseball also has fewer Black players in general: 7 percent of major leaguers were black in 2021, down from 19 percent in 1981. Brandon Jones, "73 Years After Robinson Broke Barrier, Baseball Still Struggles," *Cronkite News,* January 6, 2021; Earl Smith and Marissa Kiss, "Why Are There So Few Black American Players in MLB 74 Years After Jackie Robinson Took the Field?" *Philadelphia Inquirer,* April 1, 2021.

22. University of Chicago General Social Survey, http://www3.norc.org/GSS+ Website/. Select "whites" and "blacks" from the subject index.

23. Richard L. Harris, "For Campanis, a Night That Lived in Infamy," *Los Angeles Times,* August 5, 2008.

24. "Key Events in Marge Schott's Tenure as Owner of Cincinnati Reds," Associated Press, June 12, 1996.

25. Marc H. Morial, "Black Quarterbacks Leading More Teams in the NFL," *Huffington Post,* September 30, 2013.

26. Samuel G. Freedman, "The Year of the Black Quarterback," *New Yorker* website, January 30, 2014.

27. Roland Laird, "White Up the Middle: How Pro Football Changed the American Racial Psyche," PopMatters, January 19, 2011; Jason Reid and Jane McManus, "The NFL's Racial Divide," *The Undefeated,* April 26, 2017.

28. Kurt Badenhausen, "Highest-Paid Female Athletes 2020: 50 Years After Creation of Women's Tour, Tennis Dominates Earnings List," Forbes.com, August 17, 2020.

29. Lawrence M. Kahn, "Discrimination in Professional Sports: A Survey of the Literature," *Industrial and Labor Relations Review* 44 (1991): 395–418.

30. Kamakshi Tandon, "US Open Ratings Increase with Big Numbers During Chaotic Woman's Final," Tennis.com, September 11, 2018.

31. John J. Donohue III and James Heckman, "Continuous Versus Episodic Change: The Impact of Civil Rights Policy on the Economic Status of Blacks," *Journal of Economic Literature* 29 (1991): 1603–1643.

Chapter 7. How Do Ticket Scalpers
Make the World a Better Place?

1. Quotes from Amy Stephens come from an interview with the author on August 14, 2014.

2. "Tickets to the Colosseum," www.tribunesandtriumphs.org/colosseum/tickets-to-the-colosseum.htm.

3. Pascal Courty, "Some Economics of Ticket Resale," *Journal of Economic Perspectives* 17 (2003): 85–97.

4. Jim Armstrong, "Legal Scalping of Bruins Stanley Cup Tickets," CBS Boston, May 31, 2011, http://boston.cbslocal.com/2011/05/31/legal-scalping-of-bruins-stanley-cuptickets/.

5. Phillip Leslie and Alan Sorensen, "Resale and Rent-Seeking: An Application to Ticket Markets," *Review of Economic Studies* 81 (2014): 266–300.

6. Andrew Sweeting, "Dynamic Pricing Behavior in Perishable Goods Markets: Evidence from Secondary Markets for Major League Baseball Tickets," *Journal of Political Economy* 120 (2012): 1133–1172.

7. Ken Belson, "As Economy Sagged, Online Sports Ticket Market Soared," *New York Times,* January 14, 2011.

8. Adam Davidson, "How Much Is Michael Bolton Worth to You?" *New York Times,* June 4, 2013.

9. See, e.g., Patrick Rishe, "Dynamic Pricing: The Future of Ticket Pricing in Sports," Forbes.com, January 6, 2012.

10. Ameet Sachdev, "Baseball Teams Get Dynamic with Pricing," *Chicago Tribune,* May 12, 2013, http://articles.chicagotribune.com/2013-05-12/business/ct-biz-0512-stub-hub-20130512_1_stubhub-bleacher-ticket-ticket-reselling.

11. Quote from Larry Baer, president and CEO of the San Francisco Giants, in an email exchange with the author, April 18, 2021.

12. Gate receipt data from statistica.com.

13. Filling the stadium is more of an issue for MLB teams, where the average stadium is about two-thirds full. Owing to smaller arenas or fewer games per season, NBA, NFL, and NHL teams generally sell out or nearly sell out.

14. I am alluding here to a theory well known to economists, first espoused by the Nobel Prize winner Gary Becker. Becker suggested that he and his wife would willingly wait in line for a table at a local seafood restaurant despite the existence of a comparable but less busy restaurant directly across the street because of their (and other people's) desire to patronize businesses that have been given a social stamp of approval. Gary S. Becker, "A Note on Restaurant Pricing and Other Examples of Social Influences on Price," *Journal of Political Economy* 99 (1991): 1109–1116.

15. This is the premise for more than a few sitcom gags and real-life breakups.

16. Chris Sagers, "Why Fans Can't Win When It Comes to Buying Concert, Game Tickets," Cleveland.com, October 24, 2014.

17. Christopher Connors, "New York Yankees: The Rich and Poor Seating Divide at Yankee Stadium," Bleacherreport.com, September 21, 2012.

18. Tom Ley, "Yankees COO Defends New Ticketing Policy Like a True Rich Asshole," *Deadspin*, February 18, 2016.

19. Caleb Garling, "MLB Puts Squeeze on Sneaky Fans with App," sfgate.com, March 16, 2013.

Chapter 8. Why Should You Be Upset If Your Hometown Hosts the Olympics?

1. Richard Orange, "Berlusconi Lavishes Praise on 'Absolutely Justifiably Loved' Kazakh Leader," *The Telegraph,* December 2, 2010; Robert Mendick, "Tony Blair's Five-Million Pound Deal to Advise Kazakh Dictator," *The Telegraph,* April 23, 2016; biography on thefamouspeople.com, accessed June 11, 2016; C. J. Chivers, "Kazakh President Re-elected; Voting Flawed, Observers Say," *New York Times,* December 6, 2005; Victor Mather, "2022 Winter Games Vote Down to Two Cities and Some Major Concerns," *New York Times,* July 29, 2015; Paul Bartlett, "Disappointment for Almaty as Winter Olympics Go to Beijing," Eurasianet.org, July 31, 2015; Nadezhda Khamitova, "Almaty to Bid to Host 2022 Winter Olympics," *Astana Times,* August 21, 2013.

2. Jules Boykoff, "Beijing and Almaty Contest Winter Olympics in Human Rights Nightmare," *The Guardian,* July 30, 2015, www.theguardian.com/sport/2015/jul/30/china-kazakhstan-winter-olympics-2022.

3. "Stockholm Drops Its Bid to Host the 2022 Winter Olympic Games," BBC,

January 17, 2014; "Krakow Withdraws 2022 Winter Olympics Bid," Associated Press, May 26, 2014; "Ukraine Withdraws Bid for 2022 Winter Olympics," Associated Press, June 30, 2014.

4. Alan S. Blinder, *Hard Hearts, Soft Heads* (Perseus Books, 1988), 1.

5. John Siegfried and Andrew Zimbalist, "The Economics of Sports Facilities and Their Communities," *Journal of Economic Perspectives* 14 (2000): 103.

6. Joshua Yaffa, "The Waste and Corruption of Vladimir Putin's 2014 Winter Olympics," *Bloomberg Businessweek,* January 2, 2014.

7. Alice Ollstein, "Scott Walker to Cut $300 Million from Universities, Spend $500 Million on a Pro Basketball Stadium," thinkprogress.org, February 2, 2015; Michael Powell, "Bucks' Owners Win, at Wisconsin's Expense," *New York Times,* August 14, 2015; "Walker Signs Bill to Fund New Milwaukee Bucks Arena," WMTV Milwaukee, August 12, 2015; Don Walker, "Milwaukee Bucks Dramatically Expanding Ownership Group," *Milwaukee Journal Sentinel,* October 16, 2014; Bruce Murphy, "Cost for Taxpayers in Latest Bucks' Deal?" urbanmilwaukee.com, July 23, 2015.

8. John Duerden, "How Qatar Is Trying to Build a Team to Qualify for 2018 World Cup," ESPN.com, January 10, 2015, www.espn.com/soccer/club/name/4398/blog/post/2184455/headline.

9. Aaron Schacter, "Why Does Qatar Even Want to Host the World Cup?" Public Radio International's *The World,* June 12, 2015.

10. "Olympics 2012: A Spectacular Triumph for London," CNN, August 12, 2012, www.cnn.com/2012/08/12/opinion/hooper-london-triumph/index.html; "London 2012: How the World Saw the Olympic Games," BBC News, August 13, 2012, www.bbc.com/news/uk-politics-19238284.

11. The total cost to London for hosting was $14 billion.

12. Golden 1 Center sources: Max Resnik, "Report: Sacramento Sees Economic Boost Thanks to Golden 1 Center," KCRA-TV, October 17, 2017; Downtown Sacramento Partnership, "Golden 1 Center Fact Sheet," downloaded November 13, 2018 from www.downtownsac.org/about/reports/golden-1-center-creates-economic-spark/; Dale Kasler, "Cost of Building Golden 1 Center Just Went Up Again," *Sacramento Bee,* November 29, 2016. Arlington Stadium: Mac Engel, "Price of New Rangers Stadium Up $200 Million; New Ticket Prices and Seat Relocation Coming," *Fort Worth Star-Telegram,* October 10, 2018.

13. For details on previous studies, see Andrew Zimbalist, *Circus Maximus* (Washington, D.C.: Brookings Institution Press, 2015).

14. Paul Hirsch, "Walter O'Malley Was Right," SABR.org, accessed June 11,

2021; Gary Jeanfaivre, "Why the Whalers Left Connecticut, and Why It's Important Now," Patch.com, January 14, 2014; John Royal, "It Was Bud Adams, Not the Fans, Who Caused the Oilers Move to Nashville," *Houston Press,* February 6, 2017.

15. Roger G. Noll and Andrew Zimbalist, "Build the Stadium—Create the Jobs!" in *Sports, Jobs, and Taxes: The Economic Impact of Sports Teams and Stadiums,* edited by Roger G. Noll and Andrew Zimbalist (Washington, D.C.: Brookings Institution Press, 1997), 29.

16. Paul Dolan, Georgios Kavetsos, Christian Krekel, Dimitris Mavridis, Robert Metcalfe, Claudia Senik, Stefan Szymanski, and Nicolas R. Ziebarth, "Quantifying the Intangible Impact of the Olympics Using Subjective Well-Being Data," *Journal of Public Economics* 177 (2019).

17. The San Francisco 49ers' new stadium site in Santa Clara was also approved by voters, but with the stipulation that no public funds be spent on the construction. See the Sports and Urban Policy Initiative at Georgia State University for data on efforts to use public money to fund stadiums, https://education.gsu.edu/kh/kh researchoutreach/center-for-sport-and-urban-policy/#stadiatrack, accessed June 11, 2021.

18. Charlotte Arena: "Bobcats Unveil $265M Downtown Charlotte Arena," Associated Press, October 19, 2005. Braves Stadium: Patricia Murphy, "Tea Party Strikes Out Against the Atlanta Braves," *Daily Beast,* November 27, 2013; Tom Ley, "Braves President: Stadium Deal Had to Be Done in Secret," *Deadspin,* May 27, 2014; Matthew Pearl, "Braves President: Cobb Deal Had to Be Kept Under Wraps," 11Alive, May 22, 2014.

19. Ken Belson, "Stadium Boom Deepens Municipal Woes," *New York Times,* December 24, 2009; see also Eric Roper, "Taxes to Pay for Now-Open U.S. Bank Stadium Rebound, Thanks to Gamblers," *Minneapolis Star Tribune,* July 22, 2016.

20. Of course, one can easily argue that it is merely a quirk of American politics that deals such as those in Cobb County and Cincinnati are not considered illegal corruption.

Chapter 9. Who Wins When People Gamble?

1. Charles Curtis, "A Missed Late PAT from Browns' Cody Parkey Was a Horrible Bad Beat for Bettors," *USA Today,* October 26, 2020.

2. Todd Dewey, "Las Vegas Sportsbooks Suffer Worst Sunday of NFL Season," *Las Vegas Review-Journal,* October 25, 2020.

3. Some years are different, given that the broader population does seem to

have strong feelings about the New England Patriots, Tom Brady, and perhaps the Dallas Cowboys.

4. Thomas Johnson, "Rory McIlroy's Father Wins $171,000 Bet on His Son to Win the British Open," *Washington Post,* July 21, 2014.

5. New York State Gaming Commission, "New York State Racetracks and Applicable Takeout Rates," www.gaming.ny.gov/pdf/NYSTakeoutRates0417.pdf.

6. Sam Walker, "The Man Who Shook Up Vegas," *Wall Street Journal,* January 5, 2007.

7. Stoll uses a star-rating system whereby he assigns more stars to games about which he is most confident. He calculates his winning percentages by weighting four-star games more heavily than two-star games, but a more traditional straight-wins-and-losses calculation would still yield abnormally high win percentages from Stoll's picks.

8. Nino Bucci, "Former Junior Tennis Champion Oliver Anderson Avoids Conviction After Pleading Guilty to Match-Fixing," *Sydney Morning Herald,* May 23, 2017.

9. Justin Wolfers, "Point Shaving: Corruption in NCAA Basketball," *American Economic Review Papers and Proceedings,* May 2006, 279–283; Richard Borghesi, "A Case Study in Sports Law Analytics: The Debate on Widespread Point Shaving," *Journal of Sports Analytics* 1, no. 2 (2015): 87–89; "The Most Notorious Sports Betting Scandals of All Time," SportsHandle.com, n.d., accessed December 14, 2020.

10. Jessica Dickler, "March Madness Takes a Toll on Productivity," CNBC.com, March 18, 2018.

11. A. Blaszczynski and E. Farrell, "A Case Series of 44 Completed Gambling-Related Suicides," *Journal of Gambling Studies* 14 (1998).

12. Martin Young, Bruce Doran, and Francis Markham, "Too Close to Home: People Who Live Near Pokie Venues at Risk," The Conversation, December 5, 2013.

13. Linette Lai, "New Rules on Advance Payment of Entry Levies from August," *Straits Times,* April 4, 2019.

14. Danson Cheong and Melissa Lin, "Online Betting to Be Allowed in Next Two Months via Singapore Pools, Singapore Turf Club," *If Only Singaporeans Stopped to Think* blog, September 30, 2016.

Acknowledgments

David Oyer (my son, the hero of the chapter 1 Little League game and my Ping-Pong nemesis in chapter 5) was a major contributor to this book. He assisted with much of the research and drafted and edited several chapters. We had many discussions (and more than a few arguments) about the sports and the economics aspects of the book. Since I took David to Comiskey Park when he was four years old, it has been a great joy to experience sports with him, as both a fan and a participant. We spent time together at many Stanford sporting events, Oakland A's games, and countless Little League and other games as he was growing up. Now that he is grown, we don't get to do that as often, but he keeps me informed and amused with regular text updates about the A's and other sports topics. Spending time with David made all the research for this book far more enjoyable than it would otherwise have been.

I also spent a lot of delightful time playing and enjoying sports with my daughter, Lucy Oyer. Though my years of coaching her baseball and soccer teams did not lead to athletic stardom, she did go on to be an economics major, which seems to have prepared her well for nonathletic career success.

My wife, Kathryn Stoner, has been a wonderful companion and source of joy throughout this project. She is always encouraging, and she makes me feel lucky every day. She also knows enough economics to get by and, despite more than her share of injuries, holds her own in the sports world.

Thanks to my stepchildren, Abby and Adam Weiss, for brightening up our household at various times throughout this project. They take their athletic pursuits seriously and, hopefully, are learning some economics along the way.

Bill Frucht has been a terrific editor. I enjoyed the many conversations we had about the book, even when they inevitably devolved into lamenting the condition of the Mets. Bill was extremely patient (too patient!) and had excellent insights on the big picture of the book, as well as the little details. Speaking of patient, my agent Zoe Pagnamenta has taught me a great deal about shaping a book. Thanks, also, to Julio Cesar Franco Ardila for help with the figures.

I have had many economics colleagues, those at Stanford as well as others in the profession, who have taught me a great deal about economics over the years and have also engaged in many great discussions of sports. They are too numerous to single out here, but two are worthy of special mention. My friend and co-author Scott Schaefer has influenced my economic thinking for over twenty-five years and, more specifically, made a key point about the difference between football and baseball players that was crucial to chapter 4. Ed Lazear also made me a much better economist over the last few decades. That happened mostly through seminars, working on papers, and traditional academic pursuits, but we also spent countless hours discussing sports (with and without mentioning the underlying economics), sometimes while skiing and watching football. Sadly, Ed passed away toward the end of this project.

Josie, our faithful flat-coated retriever, was by my side throughout the entire project, including watching the Ping-Pong game in chapter 5. She was a great athlete and the most optimistic distraction from work a person could ask for, though her economics were never very good. Sadly, Josie passed away as I concluded the book. Her younger sister, Phoebe, also brings great joy to our household.

Finally, I want to thank my late mother, Alice Oyer, for all the support she gave me for over forty years. And I thank my father, Calvin Oyer, for playing sports with me and taking me to games when I was little, but never overdoing it. Neither of my parents knew much about economics, but they laid the groundwork that made this book and all my other academic endeavors possible.

Index